Managing the Risks of IT Outsourcing

Managing the Risks of IT Outsourcing

Ian Tho

Routledge
Taylor & Francis Group

LONDON AND NEW YORK

First published by Butterworth-Heinemann

First published 2005

This edition published 2011 by Routledge
2 Park Square, Milton Park, Abingdon, Oxon OX14 4RN
711 Third Avenue, New York, NY 10017, USA

Routledge is an imprint of the Taylor & Francis Group, an informa business

British Library Cataloguing in Publication Data
A catalogue record for this book is available from the British Library

Library of Congress Control Number: 200592252
A catalogue record for this book is available from the Library of Congress

ISBN 0 7506 65742

Typeset by Charon Tec Pvt. Ltd, Chennai, India

Contents

***To**
my darling wife **Cynthia**,
my loving parents **Yow Pew** and **Irene**, and
my only sister, **Su-fen**.*

About the author

Ian Tho is a practising management consultant. He has over eighteen years of international consulting experience and works with both buyers and suppliers in the area of IT outsourcing services. He is a graduate of the University of Melbourne, Australia, where he earned a BEng. He received his MBA from Monash University, Australia, and earned his PhD in the area of risks in IT outsourcing, at Deakin University, Australia. He is also a Fellow of the Australian Institute of Management.

Ian works in the area of IT outsourcing and is the National Head of Healthcare with KPMG. He works with healthcare providers, suppliers, regulators, insurance, pharmaceuticals and equipment manufacturers. He has also worked with Andersen Consulting (now Accenture) for over eleven years in its Chicago, New York, Melbourne, Paris, Singapore and Kuala Lumpur offices. Ian was the Managing Director for Asia with Datacom Asia (Outsourcing and Call Centres) where he was responsible for Datacom offices in Malaysia, Singapore, Thailand, Hong Kong, the Philippines and Indonesia. His clients include Microsoft; 3Com; Palm; Toshiba; Compaq; Dell Asia Pacific; Citibank; United Parcel Service Inc.; Carlsberg; Colgate; Shell; Jet Propulsion Laboratory, USA; Vlassic Pickles, USA; Malaysia buyer organizations; Malayan Banking; National Heart Institute, Malaysia; Telstra, Australia; the Alfred Hospital, Australia; the State Electricity Commission of Victoria, Australia; the Commonwealth Bank of Australia; and United Energy, Australia. His other clients include major organizations in healthcare, manufacturing, oil & gas and technology. Ian can be reached via e-mail at *iantho@myjaring.net*

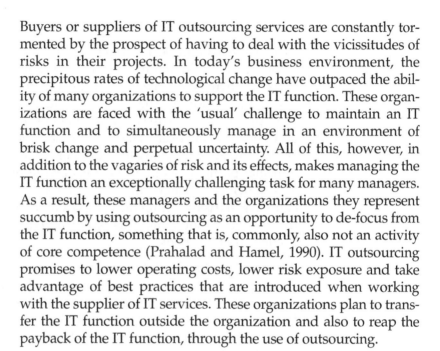

Preface

Buyers or suppliers of IT outsourcing services are constantly tormented by the prospect of having to deal with the vicissitudes of risks in their projects. In today's business environment, the precipitous rates of technological change have outpaced the ability of many organizations to support the IT function. These organizations are faced with the 'usual' challenge to maintain an IT function and to simultaneously manage in an environment of brisk change and perpetual uncertainty. All of this, however, in addition to the vagaries of risk and its effects, makes managing the IT function an exceptionally challenging task for many managers. As a result, these managers and the organizations they represent succumb by using outsourcing as an opportunity to de-focus from the IT function, something that is, commonly, also not an activity of core competence (Prahalad and Hamel, 1990). IT outsourcing promises to lower operating costs, lower risk exposure and take advantage of best practices that are introduced when working with the supplier of IT services. These organizations plan to transfer the IT function outside the organization and also to reap the payback of the IT function, through the use of outsourcing.

The term outsourcing conjures up several different meanings depending on how it is viewed. To potential and existing users of this concept, it may contain a connotation of a loss of control; and a fear that a third party would take over jobs, work and responsibility for what used to be an internal function. To others, it carries suggestions of a takeover; and to yet another group, outsourcing implies additional work that will be required to supervise additional personnel that are brought 'on-board'. Many managers, it seems, attempt to seek consolation by rejecting the concept of outsourcing altogether. Further, ideas are devised and thoughts rationalized to address this feeling of trepidation through commonly heard reasons *not* to outsource. Common reasons that may inadvertently or unintentionally be used to reinforce these concerns include, for example, 'IT outsourcing results in an unacceptable loss of control', 'intolerable increases in security issues [e.g. loss of corporate information]' or just 'undesirable increases in operational risk'. Most importantly and central to this environment, is the notion of risks introduced in Section I of this book.

Operational risks are transferred away when the IT function is outsourced, but other risk types that were formerly dormant become active and, in addition, new risks are introduced. This new uncertainty and risk has deterred many organizations considering IT outsourcing. A tool is introduced in Section II of this book that may help alleviate some of this anxiety. The tool is used in conjunction with existing risk frameworks to improve the management of risks in this environment.

Risks have seldom been addressed directly. The importance of risks, however, highlights a shift in emphasis that has taken place, as there is a realization of the significance of quantifying and understanding risks in an IT outsourcing exercise. For example, there is a grossly *uneven* experience level (experience of an IT outsourcing exercise) between the supplier and buyer that skews advantage toward the supplier. In response, it is important that participants in an IT outsourcing exercise understand and anticipate changes in the behaviour of activities that can cause harm (risks) within the complex and often inexact environment of IT outsourcing. This is illustrated in the case study in Section III of this book.

A supplier is often loath to share proprietary material and experience, possibly because of a fear that its competitors would take advantage of the way it manages its risks. As a result there are few, if any, publicized or 'shared' attempts to address the area of risks in an IT outsourcing exercise for the supplier. Buyers that need this information are not able to easily obtain it without first engaging with an outsourcing services supplier. Then again, it is the supplier that takes on the operational risks in an IT outsourcing exercise. The supplier is able to manage risk exposure, especially in the operational risk dimension, better than the buyer given its focus and dedicated resources on the IT function. So the argument continues.

This book focuses on *both* the supplier and buyer of IT outsourcing services. It guides the reader through the creation of risk profiles for both these entities; these profiles are of equal importance for a successful IT outsourcing contract and arrangement. The 'risk dimension signature', or [1]RDS instrument introduced in this book, can be deployed quickly as a tool to depict the complex

---

[1] The acronym for the risk dimension signature (RDS) used throughout this book should not be confused with the neonatal respiratory distress syndrome (RDS), also called hyaline membrane disease, which is discussed in the area of healthcare risks.

risks in any IT outsourcing environment in a simple, graphical way for both the buyer and supplier. This is used in conjunction with the more tried and proven risk management approaches. Readers will find that many concepts introduced with the RDS leverage on some of the new concepts and ways of measuring risk, which is explained in Section I. Sample approaches and instruments are mentioned as complementary tools that support the RDS. The RDS may then be used as a tool to ensure equal distribution of risks between the buyer and supplier in the IT outsourcing exercise.

Foundational concepts and terms used in IT outsourcing are explained in Section I 'Selected terms in the language of IT outsourcing'. This exercise establishes a common baseline for readers from various backgrounds, and serves to highlight nuances in the terminology, which can be quite confusing at times. With this as a background, a simplified risk measurement and management approach called the 'Measure, Understand and Mitigate', or MUM method in this book, is introduced in Sections II and III. This provides a framework for the reader to quickly capture and proactively manage risks in the IT outsourcing environment. The mathematical equations introduced in Section II represent the computation of simple risk exposure (RE). There has also been a very conscious effort to avoid the use of more-complex equations but readers who are inclined are encouraged to extend these concepts further with the author. The three sections of the book are intended to methodically introduce the reader to some of the key concepts of managing risks but importantly also, introduce the new instrument to represent the range of risks in the IT outsourcing environment. Chapter 8 provides the reader with a 'walkthrough' of a live example of an IT outsourcing exercise. Many of the concepts introduced in the book are referred to and used in the case study. With this, it is hoped that the reader is able to use the basic concepts to build better risk mitigation frameworks and enjoy more fully the concept and benefits of outsourcing.

IAN THO

Section I

Language of IT Outsourcing (ITO)

Common terms and concepts used in outsourcing

All colours will agree in the dark.
Francis Bacon (1561–1626)
English philosopher, statesman, and lawyer

The information technology (IT) function is multifaceted and complex. This complexity is increased as components and infrastructure built using new technology advances at a dizzying pace. The rate of adoption of new technology to enable organizations'[1] business processes to be differentiated from those of the competition, and, ultimately, to deliver products and services to customers, is just as feverishly brisk. IT components are, in addition, pervasive, and have become a mandatory function in most business operations.

As organizations realize the need for the IT function, they are faced with a new problem, i.e. the increasing challenge of maintaining a fully operational IT function within the organization. This is challenging because the IT function is often not a core function and continues to distract organizational activities from a main focus. Outsourcing the IT function then becomes a tantalizing prospect, which allows organizations to maintain a fully operational IT function that will have predicable outcomes and costs and that will allow them to maintain a focus on core business operations. Allowing a third party to maintain the IT function solves the difficulty. Or so it seems.

When the IT function is *combined* with outsourcing activity, the risks that are introduced form a new set of risks (or risk profile), one that is rarely observed in any other environment. For example, in this situation, elements of agency theory are observed where

---

[1] The term organization is used synonymously with generic terms like firm, enterprise, business, operation, establishment or company throughout this book.

two entities (the buyer and supplier) are contracted in an environment where there is a complex combination of tasks. This gives rise to organizational and environmental risks that are often neglected in performance measurement or payment schemes. The interaction of the environment and various factors external to either the buyer or the supplier also contributes to this complexity because of the extended duration of the contract. This combination of factors provides for a risk profile that is constructed from multiple risk types.

1.1 The need to manage risks in IT outsourcing

Managing the risks of IT outsourcing is a combination of the art of management and the science of measuring an indefinite event, i.e. risk. Risks must never be ignored but addressed proactively to ensure that their effects are never realized. Managing risks in an IT outsourcing (ITO) exercise is, in addition, not a discretionary activity. The management of risks involves active steps to reduce, to acceptable levels, the probability of an unwanted event occurring. It also requires an overall understanding of the operations, the environment and the possible effects as various factors interact.

Despite the importance of risks, many managers have either no opportunity to consider risks because of more urgent operational concerns or little understanding of how to manage something that has not yet happened. In fact, many would consider it a waste of time because it is difficult to do. In addition, current methods are inadequate for guiding and evaluating the journey that these organizations must make when working on the long-term 'deal' with a supplier and vice versa. There are many risk management tools. There are, however, few if any that allow the manager to take a snapshot of risks that occur in his/her specific environment or project. And there are fewer tools available to allow the manager to forecast and predict the behaviour of risks in the ITO environment.

If there is so much consternation over the outsourcing of the IT function, why is there significant and growing evidence for the popularity of ITO? One reason is the overwhelming number of benefits that outsourcing offers to organizations that buy and use this concept (buyers) and others that offer it (suppliers). Before taking on the concept of risks in ITO, there are some key terms and concepts where common understanding must be established.

It is very important to do this before we begin to introduce new ideas. This is especially so in this situation as expressions and nomenclature are inadvertently substituted depending on the situation. This section starts by establishing the background and highlights selected terms that are commonly used.

1.2 The practice of outsourcing

Many tasks that were once performed at home are now assumed to be more capably done by an external expert or an outside party. After all, where does one go to in order to mend one's shoes but to a cobbler; or to a clothes retailer/tailor to buy a dress; or to a barber to have one's hair cut? We now find it simply more convenient and cost-effective, and less risky, to get the products and services we need from someone who 'does it for a living'. In these situations, the risks are so minuscule that they are often not considered at all. Outsourcing of the IT function, conversely, can involve multifaceted risks and the management of a very complex set of processes, a mix of technology products and a highly trained group of people. It also involves medium- to long-term planning and a business strategy for a function that is vital for the optimal performance of the many component parts of a typical organization.

Commercially, the notion of outsourcing has also been an accepted practice for organizations such as those in the manufacturing industry. Manufacturers who practise outsourcing may choose to use third-party suppliers to provide a substantial number of components (nearly finished products) to be assembled. An example is the multinational computer manufacturer and retailer, Dell Corporation. Dell successfully assembles hardware components for its personal computers (PCs) for retail. This ensures that its PCs are often more price competitive than those of many other manufacturers. Dell purchases hard drives, monitors, memory sticks and CPUs from original equipment manufacturers (OEMs) or suppliers that manufacture and then supply the finished products to similar organizations. By sourcing the bulk of its manufacturing activity, Dell is able to secure deals that ensure better quality, on-time delivery and a more cost-effective supply chain. In this outsourcing model, products are purchased from an external party in addition to services that are provided outwith Dell. The risks of poor quality, lack of timeliness and variable cost of products become measurement criteria that Dell uses for its suppliers. This way, the outcomes of the outsourcing arrangement include products and services that are almost guaranteed to be of a minimum acceptable quality.

The experience with outsourcing is, most typically, for routine activity. There are many examples, however, where strategic outsourcing is used for 'high value' activity including the development and maintenance of cutting edge technology within very successful organizations. Outsourcing includes the delivery of products where the outcomes are goods that are of a minimum acceptable quality. Outsourcing also extends to services where the outcomes include key performance indicators (KPIs), which are measurable based on a set of predetermined criteria. In the outsourcing of product components the value is measured by the quality of the tangible goods over a period of time. Service delivery though, is often measured through a 'moment of value'. It is only during the encounter (or moment of value) between the service provider and the buyer that value is perceived.

Outsourcing is loosely defined as the use of a third party to perform tasks normally performed independently (within the organization). This idea is not new. In fact, the combination of outside expertise and internal resourcing to perform selected tasks is commonly used and has been around for a very long time. The regular use of outsourcing for the IT function, on the other hand, is a development that is relatively recent and that is in line with the use and commoditization of selected IT components over the past few decades.

Value provided in an IT outsourcing situation is generally not available until both the supplier and buyer are interacting; where the quality is subjective and quite difficult to measure fairly. The definition and subsequent measurement of value from the provision of services in the IT function therefore need to be agreed and determined via specific measurement criteria such as system downtime, transaction response times, help-desk support and other functions that support the IT function to deliver its contribution to the organizational processes. This becomes a risk factor when organizations have inadequate resources and are unprepared to measure the delivery of the supplier's services in this way. Suppliers, on the other hand, often take advantage of this inadequacy by reducing the level of service and accept some of the uneven trade in exchange for the increased possibility of unwanted events (risks) such as the delivery of unsatisfactory results for larger profit. This, however, jeopardizes both the supplier and the buyer as both parties are now confronted by higher risk exposure!

1.3 Agreeing the definition of outsourcing

The definition of outsourcing is no longer as straightforward as before. Each scenario carries unique flavours and nuances. Again, the formal definition of outsourcing is an activity where the supplier provides for the delivery of goods and/or services that would previously have been offered in-house by the buyer organization in a predetermined agreement (Elfing and Baven, 1994; Domberger, 1998). This definition implies also that outsourcing involves a buyer and supplier, where the supplier takes over a selected portion or a whole organizational function for the buyer under a set of agreed conditions.

Variations in the outsourcing process model have been presented. Further, more obvious differences in the approach become very apparent when new words or adjectives are used as modifiers of the word 'outsourcing' to convey subtle differences in meaning. The term outsourcing can be accompanied by adjectives such as 'selective', 'strategic' and 'competitive'. In addition, the function being outsourced often acts as a further descriptor of 'outsourcing'. Common examples include payroll outsourcing, IT outsourcing and sales force outsourcing. Other terms that have been used synonymously with outsourcing include terms such as out-tasking and contracting. To establish differences in process models, terms like insourcing and cosourcing have been recognized.

Further differences in definition and scope are highlighted to show the intensity of use of IT outsourcing in various settings and for a variety of purposes. In each case, the implications of risks that are noticed changes. Each change needs to be managed individually.

An important difference in the definition of outsourcing needs to be emphasized and appreciated in order to continue with the risks in this environment. This lies in the ability to distinguish process ownership from outcomes control. Early thinking defined outsourcing quite broadly, as allowing external groups to manage an organization's operations. At that time, there was no need to maintain expertise and capabilities internally where these could be obtained from a better source.

Outsourced functions can span multiple departments, units and project locations. Large outsourcing projects link the outsourced operation to other business processes in rich and often penetrating ways. This means that activities within the IT function that encompass other functions within the organization like manufacturing, design and procurement can also be covered. Metrics and incentives for the supplier become the focus of the buyer organization; measurement for reward and penalty is covered in its governance activities. The routine tasks of managing the processes within the IT function have been removed; the need for flexibility adds to this complexity. The supplier now needs to be assessed, rewarded for success or penalized for failure against this baseline.

Most organizations outsource primarily to save on overheads costs and/or induce short-term cost savings. Others do so simply because no expertise in IT exists in the organization. 'Internal' operations and administrative functions that were previously done within the organization are done outside it in outsourcing arrangements. The prevalence of IT services and their use in many organizations whose main business activity is not IT, catalysed the use of outsourcing. Supplier(s) emerged and offered benefits that the organization's internal IT organization was not able to deliver.

The definition and understanding of outsourcing in different settings, therefore, have different emphases. The emphasis on the shift in responsibility could be assumed but this point was not as clearly articulated in earlier research as in that in the later half of the 1990s. Many earlier models of outsourcing emphasized the use of an external party but there was little to describe the responsibility structures or governance of the supplier organizations. A significant portion of the literature mentions the risks involved, along with the benefits and costs; but there is insufficient detail in our understanding to describe the nature of the risks or methods used to mitigate these risks. The nature of risks that arise between the buyer and supplier when the operational functions are either contracted or outsourced is not well documented in the literature. In most of the definitions, ITO benefits the buyer through time- and cost-savings directly related to the IT function. Outsourcing is observed also as a trade-off between lower production costs (provided the supplier possesses lower-cost technology) and higher monitoring costs (Lewis and Sappington, 1991).

As the buyer provides management and supervisory content, there are restrictions imposed on the activities performed in the outsourced function. Along with this definition, a fee-for-service model is described where outsourcing services are an arrangement whereby a third-party provider assumes responsibility for performing functions at a predetermined price and according to predetermined performance criteria. It is implied that agreed terms and contractual conditions for the services performed have a service level, fee components and a deliverable that is measured against a set of measurement criteria. This extends the earlier definition to include a measurement method and a form of governance, both by the buyer and by the supplier.

Elements of this 'view' have changed since the early 1990s to include significantly more emphasis on outcomes-based agreements. The idea that a portion of responsibilities in IT can be contracted to an individual or organization on a piecemeal basis was accepted with the rise of large-scale ITO arrangements exemplified by Eastman Kodak and Xerox Corporation a decade ago. Managers questioned whether the traditional paradigm of 'owning' the factors of production is the best way to achieve competitive advantage.

In the case when responsibility and control is handed over, there is an inevitable loss of management control and responsibility over the detailed processes. Control over the IT function is relinquished voluntarily by the buyer to the supplier. There is a perception that this loss of control over the process is sometimes not adequately compensated for by increased control over the outcomes. The buyer is no longer able to directly manage all of the outsourced processes but has final control over the quality of services that are delivered through an agreement and compensation process. The outcomes of the activities in the IT function could mean defining response times for specific applications, or determining turn-around times for maintenance activities. The supplier is compensated or penalized, based on the set of agreed service levels. In this way the control over the outcomes, which is essential, remains with the buyer of the outsourcing services.

A very significant difference in meaning, however, arises when contracting is compared with outsourcing.

1.4 Contracting versus outsourcing

The terms contracting and outsourcing are often observed to be used synonymously. Although the difference is not immediately noticeable, a clear distinction needs to be made between these terms by way of control of the processes and outcomes by the buyer organization.

The difference between the different terms is important especially when risks are considered. For example, in a contracting situation, the operational processes and risks remain with the buyer of contract services. The organizational boundaries are distinct where both the buyer and supplier have no integration. The tasks, deliverables and processes are defined and agreed.

In an outsourcing situation, the processes are shifted away and become the responsibility of the supplier. In this situation the boundaries are no longer clear. The outsourced function that comprises people, processes and technology belongs to the supplier but works for, and in the interests of, the buyer organization.

Another more subtle difference is that, in contracting, there is a significant level of management effort and supervision. In outsourcing, the supplier provides a good or a service independent of the buyer management. The outsourced services are provided based on a set of performance metrices and are based on a set of outcomes rather than detailed supervision in a contracting situation. With outsourcing, the independence allows the buyer resources to be released or redeployed.

A further difference in the resourcing model using the definition, is where the processes are delegated to the supplier and almost all the staff or resources no longer belong to the buyer organization. The supplier organization fulfils this role. The motivation for streamlining processes and reducing staff resources has been shifted to the supplier. Along with this responsibility, operational risks are shifted to the supplier. The benefits to the buyer are obvious. Key benefits to the supplier come from a steady income stream over a fixed period, focus on its own core competency and an opportunity for optimal utilization of its resources. The risks that are carried are mitigated through legal agreements that set the boundaries of responsibility as well as through key factors involving reduced financial and business risks.

Process controls are 'owned by' and remain the responsibility of the buyer of the outsourcing services. The responsibility for the outcomes of the processes and ultimate ownership remains with the original buyer organization. The outside party or supplier assumes responsibility for the operations within the function, promising to deliver the outcomes previously defined by the buyer. The concept for outsourcing places emphasis on the benefits of the buyer organization through the 'removal' of non-essential or non-core competence functions from the organization.

1.5 Blurred organizational boundaries

The boundaries of the organization are redefined with the use of outsourcing. There is an observable change in the relationship of many organizations, i.e. from an external supplier of products and services to that of an entity that is networked to the buyer organization in the form of a partnership. Organizational boundaries are being redefined and expanded. The business communities today are observed to be increasingly networked. The motivation or need for new outsourcing services is integral to this new, networked community. Few single organizations can now operate independently given the need to provide more comprehensive services. The implications of the definition can be far-reaching, including the creation of virtual organizations where all activities and functions are outsourced. At the core, apart from the owners and shareholders of the organization, only the outsourcing managers remain.

Organizations, however, still struggle with the use of outsourcing to support IT. IT has been seen as the domain of a single organization because of the specialized functions it supports as well as the unique expertise required to support its operations. The ability to choose whether to outsource or not, then selecting the right IT supplier, determining the right terms, ensuring that the planned benefits are achieved and managing risks, are critical to a successful outsourcing agreement. Until the 1990s, the major drivers for outsourcing were primarily cost-effective access to specialized skills. The costs of hiring, firing, training and motivating skilled people in the area of IT representing indirect overhead costs, which are 'non-core competencies', are increasingly being outsourced.

The motivating factors and working relationships of the buyer and supplier of outsourcing services provide the background required to understand the risks as a result of 'human factors' as defined in agency theory (see subsequent section). While this book also serves to illustrate knowledge already known and published, it provides an opportunity to guide the reader to make observations of new areas that have received little or no attention in many ITO projects. These areas are highlighted as the elements of ITO are illustrated. There is a shift in emphasis that has taken place, as there is a realization of the importance of quantifying and understanding risks. This is especially so when there is an uneven experiential level between the supplier and buyer that could skew advantage toward the supplier. There are several chapters in the book that are devoted to the areas of risk that influence the decision to outsource the IT function, and the subsequent governance thereof is highlighted. The forces that determine equilibrium in the risk profiles for the buyer and supplier are of specific interest.

Finally, it is important to highlight a key difference in terminology and concept between what may appear to be virtually the same at first, but which in fact have significant differences. Differences in emphasis are discussed next.

1.6 Differences in emphasis

Risks are observed to derive from the way an exercise is managed, the very definition of the term outsourcing and the use of IT within the organization. The transfer of risks is different in one scenario compared to another, and the buyer/supplier relationships are different. In addition, changes in the process model and related risk profiles depend on this definition of outsourcing.

Risk transfer difference

The risks previously borne by the buyer in a contracting exercise for the management and supervision of a particular function are relinquished to the supplier in an outsourcing exercise. In the context of evaluating the risks and risk exposure of the supplier and buyer organizations, risks are transferred from the buyer to the supplier along with processes, assets and personnel management. The majority, if not all, of the buyer's resources are no longer required and will no longer exist. In another outsourcing/contracting situation the work functions might still belong to the outsource supplier and the operations risk exposure still remains with the buyer organization.

The reductions in operational risks when a function is removed do not mean that the total risk exposure of the buyer organization has decreased. There are increased legal, financial and strategic risks as a result of the outsourcing exercise. The agreement between the buyer and supplier organization is a source of new risks. The variation in emphasis shifts operational risk to the supplier; this changes the relationship between the buyer and supplier. In addition there are the implications of the relationship between the buyer and supplier organizations to consider.

Buyer/Supplier relationship difference

The relationship between the buyer and supplier changes with the type of contract or commercial arrangement. Assuming the supplier is able to deliver the same activities as the buyer but at a lower cost, the difference in costs translates to a profit margin for the supplier. In the outsourcing model discussed in the previous sections, the supplier is no longer required to follow the processes previously owned by the buyer. In this way, the supplier is now free to make modifications to the original process, motivated by profitability.

The buyer and supplier relationship forms a key component that will make the outsourcing arrangement either a success or a failure. The questions that are posed remain relevant in a dynamic buyer–supplier relationship. Some key examples include questions like: What prevents the supplier from compromising on quality and delivering lower-quality work to derive higher margins (gains)? How can the buyer manage the activities of the supplier to ensure that the promises of quality services are delivered? What is the buyer going to do in order to manage the supplier, who will be motivated only to reduce its own costs? Will the supplier's methodology be acceptable to the buyer? How is the supplier going to manage its risks and where are the risks going to come from?

This raises the need to have ongoing supplier and buyer governance procedures. When considering the relationship, each party (the buyer and supplier) needs to consider managing their individual risk profiles to within acceptable risk tolerance levels.

As the buyer and supplier interact, components of agency theory apply. In the governance of outsourcing, both the buyer and supplier work in an agency environment. There are various models propounded by researchers and practitioners for managing this relationship. The 'potential contract' relationship model addresses the organizational needs of control and flexibility. Here, commercial arrangements including multiple supplier contracts, joint ventures, individual and joint-venture spin-offs, consortia and shared service structures re-emphasize the importance of the quality of supplier–buyer relationships.

Changes in process model difference

'Changes' in this section refers to the specific process differences between outsourcing and contracting. To examine the alternative sources of risks within the ITO exercise, changes in the process model are reviewed. The need for control over the processes being outsourced stems from a variety of other requirements, like the need to maintain quality in the processes as well as control of the risks. Managers of organizations are anxious when key functions are performed outwith the organization. At the same time, these managers require flexibility in moulding the services in order to deliver optimum service. In a situation where maximum control and flexibility is needed, the buyer and supplier relationship is in a state of close partnership (Figure 1.1).

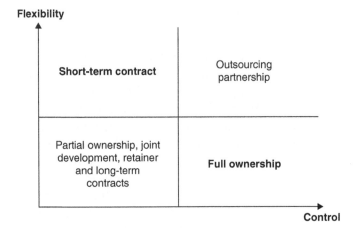

Figure 1.1
Relationship between buyer and supplier in a contract setting (Tho, 2004)

In situations where the need for control is low and flexibility is high, short-term contracts are suitable. Conversely, in situations where the need for flexibility is low and the need for control is high, a full ownership contract is the overriding factor in the agreement. In between these extremes lie alternative arrangements involving partial ownership, joint development, retainer and long-term contracts.

As was noted earlier, to the buyer, there is concurrently greater control over the outcomes of processes as the supplier of services is directly accountable to the buyer for the outcomes of the processes. The benefit to the buyer is, then, a smaller organization, reduced attention to extraneous processes and stricter control over the critical outcomes. When engaged in an outsourcing exercise the buyer organization utilizes the external supplier's investments, innovations, and specialized professional capabilities. The supplier provides multiple organizations with the services and benefits from economies of scale. This would be prohibitively expensive to achieve for any single organization operating independently. These concepts support the view that activities such as the IT capability, for which the organization has no crucial strategic need, could be and should be outsourced.

An external supplier that can provide superior services is used where service quality improvement, the need for strategic flexibility and the focus on core competencies are primary concerns for sourcing decisions. The need for quality services and improved operational efficiencies is consistent and remains as the core reason to outsource the IT function (on core competency and economies of scale). In addition, the strategic requirement to focus on core competency has been an additional catalyst for outsourcing services. Figure 1.2 is an attempt to summarize some of the views expressed here.

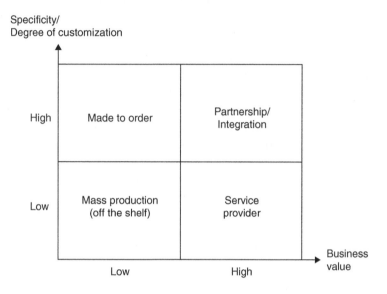

Figure 1.2
A model for outsourcing relationships

If the ability to provide business value is mapped against the flexibility or degree of customization required, then several other variants of the relationship appear (see Figure 1.2). High business value and high customization (top right quadrant) is delivered only when there is a close partnership or integration; much like an in-house process unit.

There would be very little business value if the services were mass produced (bottom left quadrant). In a service provider model (bottom right quadrant) where the contracts are made based on commoditized services, business value would be high but relatively lower than in an integrated or partnership model. In a made to order situation (top left quadrant), business value is still low but this would be compensated for by a higher degree of fit, or specificity. The customer or buyer would then have a more-tailored business solution. The model that provides the maximum return is the integrated solution where, together with high specificity or an ability to customize, the services to the buyer organization have a high degree of business value. This outsourcing partnership arrangement is characterized by a constant transfer of operations risk between the buyer and supplier.

Outsourcing is an almost ubiquitous concept, which is used in different scenarios and in different industries to achieve business benefits including an impact not only on direct cost but on the business and strategic drivers. The strategic impact involves value creation through strategic relationships, freeing up investments, increased flexibility and scalability, and the ability to build on strategic capabilities. For some organizations with high specificity, the significant nature of inseparable supplementary services may warrant the need for internal sourcing to ensure tighter quality control.

The quality of the final deliverable or outcome is dependent on the supplier being able to deliver an improved service compared to services that have been performed in-house. To do this efficiently, suppliers have an advantage over the buyer organization. For example, the supplier has more access to competence in new technologies, access to better IT professionals, and better processes for IT integration and development. In all these models, however, there is still scant detail on how the risks are transferred between the buyer and supplier, what the risks are, when they occur and the extent to which each party can tolerate the risks before an existing relationship is irreparably severed (as a result of the outcomes of these risks).

1.7 Process changes

The processes that are enabled by the use of the IT function are changing and complex. Those that are driven by IT, change as a result of this. Figure 1.3 represents an attempt to summarize some of the dynamics of this change.

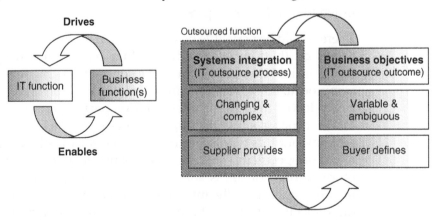

Figure 1.3 Business functions/processes are the drivers for information technology (IT) development. IT in turn, enables the creation of more-efficient business processes, including 'outsourcing processes' (Tho, 2004)

An attempt made to illustrate the coexistence of IT and business processes in a tightly linked relationship demonstrates interdependence between business processes and the IT function. The organization's business objectives *drive* the IT function in order to deliver the expected outcomes – where the IT function *enables* successful outcomes.

Figure 1.3 consists of two halves. On the left, the illustration shows the IT function enabling a group of business functions. The business functions, in turn, drive the design of the IT function. This continuous loop identifies the changes that constantly occur in an organization's IT support function.

On the right, the IT function is outsourced. The outsourced provider controls the systems integration (SI) process. It is both changing and complex because of the need to satisfy the business function requirements of the buyer organization as well as the profit motives of the supplier organization. On the far right of the diagram, the business objectives have now become the outcome that is required when the IT function is outsourced. The buyer defines these processes and sets appropriate standards that need to be achieved by the IT function that has been outsourced to the supplier. The objectives are often variable and ambiguous because of the business conditions that drive the organization.

Along with the changes in IT, new business processes emerge and need to be designed. New platforms, operating systems, networks and applications are driven by changes in the competitive business environment. This influences business operations as information needs become more urgent. As competitive pressures mount, business objectives drive the development of further IT components. The changes in processes and functions are in turn driven more quickly by the use of more-efficient IT components.

The extremely fast rate of change of IT components creates a reversing effect. IT is the catalyst for process change and outsourcing. Instead of the business functions driving change (see Figure 1.3), the direction of the arrows now shows the reverse. Outsourcing processes rely on IT for access to organizational information accurately, quickly and cost-effectively. It is recognized that IT facilitates the reduction of transaction costs without increasing transaction risks. This in turn drives further outsourcing activities.

In addition to illustrating the differences in meaning of the concepts in outsourcing, it is equally important to collectively agree some of the motivating factors of the buyer and supplier organizations in order to discuss the risks that both these parties face. The fundamental criteria for buyer and supplier motivation are the acceptance of the ITO exercise and the benefits derived.

1.8 Acceptance of information technology outsourcing (ITO)

A primary objective of a buyer of ITO services is very often to reduce operational risk. The risks that accompany the operations are moved outside the organization when the IT function is moved away. ITO is then a way to reduce operational risks as well as manage IT costs while, at the same time, retaining the benefits of the IT function that is so crucial, within the control of the buyer organization. Much of the argument to outsource the IT function also arises as current management ideology emphasizes the need to optimize the organization's resources; the notion of being able to completely remove the need to maintain an in-house IT function while being able to enjoy the benefits of the services and use of a world-class IT capability (supplied by an external 'expert') is a very tempting proposition.

Many commercially available reports agree and predict that large outsourced IT markets will develop. These global markets are collectively expected to hit approximately US$1 trillion over the next 5 to 6 years (or by the year 2010) as many more organizations choose to implement ITO. The reach and richness of this influence is significant. The acceptance of outsourcing of the IT function provides some indication of the level of satisfaction that organizations have with the concept, the benefits derived and also importantly, the ability to manage the risks within this environment.

The IT function is more ubiquitous than any other we have seen. Early in the 1980s many tasks involving the use, maintenance and upgrade of computer systems required knowledge only privy to a few. There was no choice but to employ specialist help to maintain the IT function within the organization. The use of IT, however, has become prevalent over the last two decades. The machines or computers that enable IT to function have become universal, and much easier to use and maintain; yet, the same computers have become more complex. As such, it is suggested that the influence of risks on so many significant parts of the organization has hitherto not been experienced to this level of severity and extent.

For the most part, however, the published experience with the outsourcing of the IT function indicates a dismal track record. Also, it has been suggested that as the nature of IT is not consistent across organizations, industry groups and country settings, the acceptance and use of outsourcing of the IT function has created further confusion. The risks are not easy to measure let alone understand; it is no wonder then that many organizations experience severe anxiety when considering the option to outsource the IT function.

Early adopters and failures

Substantial market size does not necessarily imply that there are satisfied buyers. Nearly seventy per cent of organizations that have outsourced say that they are unhappy with one of more aspects of their suppliers. International research shows that only about half of ITO contracts deliver the previously promised twenty to thirty per cent cost savings. Even back in the early 1990s, a considerable number of organizations expressed dissatisfaction with outsourcing (Currie and Willcocks, 1997). Other studies indicate that fifty-three per cent of organizations attempt to renegotiate the original terms of the contract with their partners, and that twenty-five per cent of those renegotiations end in the termination of the relationship (Caldwell, 1997). Other estimates show that outsourcing clients spend fifteen per cent of their IT budget on litigation (Goodridge, 2001).

The Gartner report (Murphy, 2004) mentioned that, by 2005, there would be a sixty per cent probability that seventy-five per cent of organizations that fail to recognize and mitigate risk throughout the outsourcing life-cycle will fail to meet their outsourcing goals because of misaligned objectives, unrealized expectations, poor service quality and cost overruns. While many of the data justify this fear of outsourcing, a view can be taken from an alternative perspective. The qualitative evidence of ITO implementation displays symptoms of an industry in turmoil. The track record that is available has its share of success and failures. Much of the literature on the benefits to the supplier, for example, has not been published or is not available. Could it be that the information remains a source of competitive advantage and hence is being kept 'secret'? Could it be that this fearful notion of impending failure is, just possibly, exacerbated and made to proliferate by an unintentionally one-sided press, by research papers and by word of mouth? Whatever the case, the elements of risk of information-loss exist. Risks need to be measured, understood and then mitigated to ensure that the benefits of ITO have the best chance of being reaped.

There are two sides to this scenario. Managers deciding to use ITO are often very optimistic. These managers have been observed to make decisions to outsource based on a best-case scenario, i.e. based on their individual expectations or based on the instructions of their superiors (Saunders *et al.*, 1997). This confidence raises expectations. This has been observed to result in unpredictable events, the majority (relative to the optimistic views) of which yield poor results as compared to the case where the risks are anticipated and managed.

Other managers hesitate when faced with the proposition to outsource the IT function. This hesitation is expressed as a fear, and, as a result, also a hesitance to lose control over the daily operations and routine use of the IT function. This innate fear is often a result of an absence of a clear understanding of the possible undesirable outcomes (or risk) that may result from a loss of control over the management of the detailed activities in the IT function. With this, unnecessary steps are taken to regain control from the supplier, frequently having disastrous consequences. This is often called organizational risk.

1.9 Benefiting from ITO

It is clear that competition for access to growing amounts of information over geographically disparate locations, over shorter periods has been a significant inducement for the need to maintain a more significant and reliable IT capability within the organization. The efficiency and effectiveness of an organization's IT function has become a source of competitive differentiation. In the mid-1980s, Michael Porter (1985) propounded and championed the concept of competitive advantage through lower costs and differentiation. He parleyed the concept of the value chain, the pervasive nature of IT in the value chain, and its use as a source of differentiation. As the IT function is inextricably connected to many parts of the value chain, it becomes a vital component that differentiates the organization's products and services from those of its competitors (Blaxill and Hout, 1991; Teng *et al.*, 1995).

There is a noticeable increase in acceptance of outsourcing of the information technology (IT) function as a management tool to defray some of the pressures of increasing competition by achieving competitive advantage through lower costs and the ability to deliver improved IT support. The decision to outsource the IT function is made primarily because it benefits the buyer of ITO services and also provides benefits for the supplier of the same services in a win–win situation. This is also commonly referred to as the 'make' or 'buy' decision. The decision is not easy to make as the elements involved in the decision-making process are often varied and peculiar to the specific environment and organizational needs. There are, however, commonalities that often form the main reasons why organizations choose to out-source the IT function to a third-party supplier. These common-alities primarily derive from opportunities to benefit from specialization and then from economies of scale and economies of scope within the context of the IT function. These concepts are discussed in greater detail, with specific reference to ITO, in the next chapter. All these elements have been demonstrated to reduce cost and sharpen the organization's focus on the stra-tegic IT function.

Outsourcing has been increasingly used to provide a tangible means and path for many organizations to reduce costs and improve the quality of their products, among other consider-ations. In addition, it is used as a tool for strategic advantage. A summary, from this research, of the two key strategic reasons for outsourcing the IT services function includes the organization's need to:

1. acquire additional *competence* – the organization cannot sup-port or easily acquire support for the IT function; and,
2. move to be more *competitive* – the supplier of IT services has lower costs and faster availability for the IT function, which is viewed as a critical but directly substitutable item.

In addition, the key strategic reasons for not seeking a supplier include the protection and retention of:

1. *Intellectual property* – processes and information contained within the IT function provide proprietary or competitive information that is crucial to the organization's performance (Venkatesan, 1992); and,
2. *Market differentiation* – the organization should retain what matters most to the customer or what differentiates its product(s) in the market-place.

The benefits of ITO are often already quite obvious to the indi-vidual involved with the exercise. Some of these benefits

Table 1.1   Buyer and supplier interests in outsourcing

Buyer (business objectives aligned with supplier metrics)	Supplier (supplier rewarded for increased value)	Joint
• Well-defined objectives • Internal benchmarking • Evaluation rewards & penalties • Control • Accountability • Cost savings • Improved performance • Improved profitability	• Service level targets • Financial target costs • Revenue growth • Objective evaluation • Additional profit • Contract extensions	• Increase value relationship • Initiative creation • External benchmarking • Scenario planning

accrued by the buyer and supplier are summarized in Table 1.1. Similarly with any business transaction, all the benefits have related risks. Organizations that buy services that support the IT function commonly do so to secure greater cost savings and improve performance and, hence, enhance profitability. Along with this are to be considered financial, operational and technical risk factors, which are discussed in the next chapter. As a purchaser of ITO services the buyer organization is able to define the supplier accountability and have control over the outcomes through a series of legal contracts and agreements. Control is also enhanced through an incentive programme whereby the supplier's rewards and penalties are based on a set of predefined and agreed benchmarks. These characteristics reduce the risk of errant outcomes often observed in a less structured arrangement (see Contracting). The risk of poor governance exists as the contract duration of an ITO exercise is often long and spans multiple financial periods.

The supplier organization also benefits synergistically from the ITO exercise. As the supplier provides services, it derives benefits from economies of scale (see later). This source of efficiency naturally leads to additional profit for each unit of work performed. A major reason a supplier organization offers ITO services, however, is often always that a predictable income stream is established over long, contracted periods of time. Again, this makes the procurement of work processes a great deal more efficient. At the same time, the supplier is able to focus on activities of core competency (Prahalad and Hamel, 1990; Quinn, 1993); this only serves to enhance the efficiency of its operations. As it delivers increasingly efficient operations, it is rewarded through contract extensions and additional profit from increasing margins.

The organizations involved are legally obliged to follow a series of agreed benchmarks and are equally motivated to improve these benchmarks. Jointly, both the buyer and supplier organizations benefit from this synergistic relationship wherein each organization exists to deliver common services. This leads to a common motivation to increase value in the relationship and the value of the products and services delivered as a result of the relationship. This combination also provides an environment wherein both parties initiate new processes, creating more value for common benefit.

While the benefits remain quite obvious, the risks that shadow each of the benefits often remain unnoticed, until the risks reveal themselves as an undesirable outcome. The causes of undesirable outcomes are obscured in the scenario where each party is so tightly engaged in an environment conducive only to productivity. The experienced manager would understand that each of the readily observable benefits carries major risk elements. In order to examine the risks, some of the commonly accepted definitions of risk in the ITO environment are introduced here.

The balance of the benefits and the risks or costs needs to be clear when an organization decides to outsource its IT function. This is, however, seldom the case especially when the risks are difficult to understand, let alone quantify. Such an organization is susceptible to 'normal operating risks' and to even more risks because of the interplay of newly created forces that arise during the long-term partnerships that come into being in an outsourcing arrangement. Additional influencing factors or causes of the risks derive from a wide range of possibilities, including failed relationships, malicious action, purposeful or inadvertent contractual obligations, and natural, man-made disasters.

Supplier benefits

The argument on core competence (discussed in detail in Chapter 2) is that the greater specialization in the provision of services, through outsourcing, the greater the benefits of economies of scale (also discussed in Chapter 2). As activities are shared and contributing cost elements are increased, the natural economies of scale are realized. As costs are known to be a major consideration in the decision to outsource the IT function, the realization of benefits from economies of scale becomes critical. Until the 1990s, the main drivers for outsourcing IT were primarily cost-effective access to specialized skills and avoidance of building in-house IT skills. Cost-savings and freedom to focus upon core business are still major reasons for outsourcing.

Common (buyer and supplier) benefits

The intent of the ITO services is to deliver greater capacity for flexibility, especially in the purchase of rapidly developing new technologies and the myriad components of complex systems within the IT function. Through economies of scale, benefits from a significantly larger pool of resources are available to both the supplier and buyer of outsourcing services.

Outsourcing also decreases the product/process design cycle time, and the suppliers provide best-in-class service contributing to greater depth and sophisticated knowledge in specialized areas. Outsourcing makes the full utilization of external suppliers' investments, innovations, and specialized professional capabilities available to the buyer, which would be prohibitively expensive to replicate otherwise.

ITO provides organizations with greater capacity for flexibility, especially in the context of the purchase of rapidly developing new technologies, new people, and myriad components of complex systems.

Buyer benefits

An organization's ability to compete successfully is based on consistent, superior performance, or the development of assets of high specificity that create value through differentiation. Many organizations rely on the ability to deliver 'better' and/or 'cheaper' than the competition in order to successfully capture and hold a market. When internal performance (within the organization) falls below the performance levels of external suppliers a 'surrogate' arrangement is observed to deliver immediate benefits. Many benefits of the surrogate arrangement derive from economies of scale.

As organizations faced with intense competitive pressures are forced to shed non-essential functions, outsourcing becomes the driving force behind the 'virtual corporation'. The search for greater flexibility and rapid changes in technology, and the emphasis on concentrating on core competencies have been cited as major drivers for the upsurge in outsourcing activity. The virtual organization appears less a discrete organization and more an ever-varying cluster of common activities in the midst of a vast fabric of relationships. The network of partners itself is seen as a sequence of value-adding activities in a value chain. The well-put case for an organization to outsource its IT function has a very significant influence. The question is now not whether to outsource; rather, what and how to outsource the activities which do not contribute to these objectives.

Suppliers are able to provide a level of responsiveness through new technologies that undermine the need for the vertically integrated organization and achieve economies of scale. This translates into benefits for the buyer. A network of suppliers provides the organization with the ability to adjust the scale and scope of its production capability (upward or downward), at a lower cost, to changing demand conditions and at a rapid rate. This creates greater flexibility than is the case for the vertically integrated organization.

The benefits of outsourcing any service, identified via surveys a few years ago (1998) conducted by the Outsourcing Institute of the top 10 reasons why organizations buy outsourcing services for their operations, fall into the following areas:

- Reduction and control of operating costs.
- Improvement in organizational focus.
- Gain of access to world-class capabilities.
- Free internal resources for other purposes.
- Resources are not available internally.
- Accelerated re-engineering benefits.
- Function difficult to manage/out of control.
- Capital funds made available.
- Shared risks.
- Cash infusion.

We have referred to the organizations that use and supply ITO services as separate entities. In terms of legal setup, corporate governance, responsibility to shareholders, corporate structure and the like, these organizations are indeed separate. When two organizations engage in an ITO exercise, however, the processes that link both participants make them more logically appear as a single entity. This concept can be confusing as the boundaries that define each organization are now blurred.

1.10 Outsourcing models

There already exist numerous outsourcing models. Additional models are constantly being formulated as the requirements of each ITO agreement differ. The need to create new models to describe each flavour and variation is nevertheless important as it serves to highlight also the variations in effort, measurement of risk and treatment of the outcomes. Transformational outsourcing, for example, provides for a set of partners who have a considerable stake in the game, and often that means sharing both risk and reward. To make the transformation work, the commercial agreement must fund the necessary investment at the best possible cost of capital and simultaneously motivate the outsourcing partners' commitment by aligning goals. This is quite different from the outsourcing of the commoditized IT function.

Evans and Wurster (2000) describe the new economics of information where information can be replicated at almost zero cost (in contrast to the economics of items that incur manufacturing costs). The evolving technological capabilities for sharing and using information are transforming business definitions, industry definitions and competitive advantage where information is the glue that holds the value chains and supply chains together. This observation impacts on the way organizations are structured. Informational value chains become separate from physical value chains, releasing tremendous economic value. When the trade-off between richness and reach is no longer tenable, traditional structures and relationships throughout the business world begin to deconstruct (as new level of richness and reach are attainable). Processes that used to work within an organization and between organizations, as well as between organizations and their customers, are being transformed.

There are observable changes as organizations deconstruct. The same authors, Evans and Wurster, talk about deconstruction that occurs as organizations dismantle and re-form traditional business structures. Competitive advantage is de-averaged as competition escalates. Information businesses take on new value. New opportunities arise for physical businesses. Wholesalers, retailers and distributors are disintermediated. Navigators emerge and incumbents are challenged. The organized supply of competency-based services and products, however, has matured as an industry over the past two decades. Information is becoming increasingly accessible across time and space. People, and more importantly our collective knowledge, are becoming increasingly interlinked via high-speed networks, databases and active data collection devices. Individual, group and organizational relationships have drastically changed. In this environment, however, the stage is set for optimal use of outsourcing services given the ability to seamlessly share information.

Very often suppliers of 'outsourcing' services have access to a very limited amount of information, just sufficient to complete the work at hand. For example, incomplete personnel data are shared, just sufficient to complete regular payroll for payroll outsourcing. If information on recruitment, personnel evaluation, staffing, strategy and planning were available, the supplier can more proactively plan for changes in resourcing, provision of supplies, staffing for its own delivery and investments in infrastructure.

Outsourcing types

Outsourcing has been used in a variety of ways, those which involve combinations of partnership agreements and duration, payment structures, and service as well as product content. Some of the characteristics of the outsourcing genre are discussed here.

The adjectives that describe outsourcing activity are as varied as the combinations of outsourcing models that are present. Some common types of outsourcing models include total outsourcing (with sole supplier), multiple-supplier sourcing (or with prime contractor and partners), joint venture/strategic alliance sourcing and insourcing. It is logical also to assume that there is prolific variation on the themes given the differences in each organization's situation. Alternative structures include matrix-type models, based on the interrelationships of core competencies and organization activities, to assist managers with outsourcing decisions. The effort to reduce costs and exploit new channels of distribution like the Internet reveal new organizational forms. Cost-savings and freedom to focus upon core business, however, are still major reasons for outsourcing.

Literature suggests the buyer sourcing choices between carrying out activities in-house, or under 'hierarchical governance', and outsourcing them and placing them under market governance through cost–benefit reasoning, is determined by the relative costs of production and transactions. Economic analysis of the provision of outsourcing services is limited. It does not, for example, account for the organization's management capability to structure and manage co-operative relationships crucial to the effective working of outsourcing arrangements. Further, it does not take into account the effectiveness (as opposed to the cost) of acquiring the necessary information. This supports the assumption that a closely integrated network of organizations will perform better. Learning through alliances can complement endogenous learning to create new competencies.

The extent to which such strategies are successful is not always clear; for instance it was found that there is no direct effect of strategic technology alliances on economic performance in general. However, it was established that in high-tech industries research-oriented strategic technology alliances are associated with higher economic performance. It is often also suggested that complementarity is a major driver of partnering behaviour (Hagedoorn, 1993). This suggests that a strategy aimed at creating a rather broad set of alliances that are complementary to the already existing capabilities could have a more positive effect on organizational performance than the formation of alliances that parallel existing capabilities.

The concept was for basic (more routine) operations to be performed on behalf of the organization to the extent that they could be carried out by machines or computers. Some have envisaged scenarios where mass-produced or 'off-the-shelf' products would eliminate the need for services, whether in-house or externally sourced.

Complete/Selective outsourcing

Theoretically, the whole organization can be outsourced. The rationale for total outsourcing is to enable the client to concentrate on its core business activities, thus leaving the supplier to manage core business functions more efficiently. Total ITO, as opposed to selective outsourcing, is generally thought to have begun in 1989, when Kodak outsourced its entire IT function to IBM and a few smaller suppliers. In the early 1990s approximately twenty major corporations followed suit, but the general view in the business world was that this total ITO exercise was a mistake.

On the other hand, there are some who argue against complete outsourcing. Fowler is an advocate of the case against complete outsourcing (Fowler, 1997). He argues that there is a significant proportion of personnel work that is central to the culture and strategic objectives of the organization that can be undertaken effectively only by the organization itself. Hence, personnel should be retained, at least in part, as an integral part of the business. Further, the occurrence of situations such as industrial disputes may be quite unpredictable; these issues require immediate action. It is all but impossible to specify such tasks precisely enough to contract them out, or to find an external provider that can guarantee the instant and informed response they require.

Selective outsourcing involves outsourcing portions of the process, rather than the process in its entirety. The strategy of selective outsourcing where discrete services or functions are sourced to a group of best-of-breed service providers is seen as an appealing alternative to large-scale, single-supplier arrangements, which are frequently characterized by excessive fees, unrealized cost-savings, ill-defined contractual terms and service levels, and inflexibility in response to changing business requirements. This is a strategy to mitigate certain of the risks that were inherent in the 'deal'. Half-measures, however, would prevent the buyer from achieving best practice and introduce further risks.

Some of the advantages of selective outsourcing include relatively lower switching costs and lower probability of failure. It is also suggested that it is suited for processes which are smaller in scope. The disadvantages, however, include the lowered ability of the supplier to affect the buyer's business objective or leverage economies of scale. This appears as a low-risk, low-return strategy; it would also lack the strategic perspective and benefits of outsourcing. Examples include sole-sourcing and individual out-tasking.

Keiretsu

So far the concepts and models of outsourcing have focused on observations from Western-type cultures. The practice of *maquiladora* between the United States and Mexico involves work being outsourced to factories in a location where the cost of labour is low. A hybrid concept, which is found to be closely related to the concepts of relinquishing or handing over control of a function, found in an Eastern-type culture, is *Keiretsu*. *Keiretsu* refers to a uniquely Japanese form of corporate organization. Although *keiretsu* is not, strictly speaking, an outsourcing model, it is discussed here for the sake of completeness. A grouping or family of affiliated organizations that form a tight-knit alliance to work toward each other's mutual success, forms a *keiretsu*. The *keiretsu* system is also based on an intimate partnership between government and businesses. A *keiretsu* represents an intricate web of relationships that links banks, manufacturers, suppliers and distributors with the Japanese government. The *keiretsu* model mirrors many outsourcing partnership models that have been put together. From here, however, the concepts seem to diverge.

Horizontal *keiretsu* are headed by major Japanese banks and include the 'Big Six', i.e. Mitsui, Mitsubishi, Sumitomo, Fuyo, Sanwa, and Dai-Ichi Kangyo Bank groups. The two models most often described are the vertical and horizontal *keiretsu*. The vertical *keiretsu* are industrial groups connecting manufacturers and parts suppliers or manufacturers, wholesalers and retailers. Examples of the vertical *keiretsu* include Toyota, Nissan, Honda–Matsushita, Hitachi, Toshiba and Sony. Distribution *keiretsu*, a subgroup of vertical *keiretsu*, control much of Japanese retailing, determining what products will appear in stores and showrooms and at what price.

These organizations would engage in cost-sharing with smaller suppliers much akin to the outsourcing model discussed. The sharing of costs is via various types of investment in customizing assets and supplier support services and training.

Unlike vertically integrated organizations which deploy certain skills from market to market, Japanese automotive organizations are structured around 'mother organizations'. The participating organization aims to design and assemble products through a number of independent suppliers and alliance partners, but without owning such satellite organizations. This long-standing and successful subcontracting culture is based on inter-organizational co-operation. The model, however, does reflect the outsourcing structure that is practised outside Japan. The relationship, however, carries expectations, as the group of 'buyers' and 'suppliers' work in a *keiretsu* in symbiosis, involving mutual gain. This relationship is cultivated at a subsequent stage in an outsourcing relationship.

The divergence in concepts merely demonstrates and confirms that diversity in hybrid models exist. The range of options is theoretically unending. What remains central in the theme of outsourcing, however, is the commercially viable arrangement between the buyer and supplier of these services. In the case of IT this is complicated by the fact that the very nature of IT is evolving so quickly.

1.11 Outsourcing partnerships

Again, the ability to connect quickly and meaningfully with business partners and customers in order to rapidly improve the quality of goods and services is becoming the competitive imperative. Consequently, organizations are rapidly 'devolving' from being self-contained and vertically integrated to being more virtual entities that rely on business partners to fulfil major parts of their supply and value chain requirements.

While partnership arrangements vary considerably in their operations, from flexibly defined, formal contacts, to loose strategic initiatives, they also encompass the provision of shared risk and benefits. Organizations with large, centralized departments that undertake most of the work in-house may also outsource specific applications to specialist suppliers. Alternatively, other organizations may seek to enter into multiple/selective sourcing contracts with a range of external suppliers to seek to reduce their internal facilities over time. The relationships so formed are described as 'strategic alliances' or 'strategic partnerships'.

The options range from handing over complete IT operations, to pay-as-you-go for single application outsourcing. Notwithstanding the options, deep business ties and dependencies are often forged between the two organizations, and while partnerships can solve some workload issues, the biggest problem they face is how to make these relationships more painless and more collaborative. However, there exist several disadvantages to adopting outsourcing strategies. These include becoming dependent on outside suppliers for services, failing to realize the expected hidden cost savings, losing control over critical functions, having to face the prospect of managing relationships that go wrong and lowering the morale of permanent employees.

Figure 1.4 summarizes the range and intensity of relationships. In the illustration, the intensity of the relationship is plotted

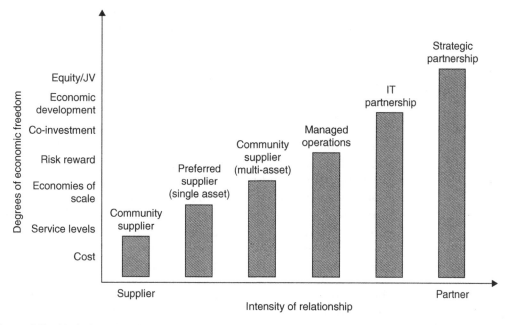

Figure 1.4   Variations in relationships in the outsourcing of the IT function

against the type of partnership both the supplier and buyer have agreed on. The type of partnering relationship is often also described by suppliers as the degree of economic freedom. This could be a loose arrangement at one end of the scale, such as a price for service or cost model. At the other end of the scale, the supplier could be linked to the buyer in the form of a joint venture (JV) where both parties have a stake in the arrangement. The partnership agreement controls the degree of economic freedom that either the buyer or supplier has during the period agreed at that time. There are multiple options available, of which six variations are listed in Figure 1.4. The idea behind the illustration is that in a strategic partnership arrangement, there are also often very tight economic arrangements that bind both parties into delivering high levels of service and that have very significant economic considerations. At the other end of the scale, where it is very much like a contracted situation (see Contracting versus Outsourcing), the model is that of a community supplier that provides single services for a fee.

To this end, service levels are occasionally used to manage supplier operations. As the partnership relationship develops and more trust exists in the relationship, a preferred supplier status materializes with either one or multiple assets. It is common to see a risk–reward type compensation structure materialize as the supplier is trusted to deliver and can occasionally act on its own initiative. Economies of scale arise as the resources and processes are controlled by the supplier. At this point, there is joint investment and joint responsibility for the outcomes of the function that has been outsourced. In a partnership situation, at the far right of the figure, there is equity in the outcomes and an integrated delivery effort by both the supplier and buyer comes into being. At this stage, almost all the benefits are observed in a synergistic business environment.

A 'potential contract' relationship model addresses the organizational needs of control and flexibility. Many new arrangements have emerged in the late 1990s, exemplified by multiple supplier contracts, joint ventures, individual and joint venture spin-offs, consortia and shared service structures. The importance of the quality of supplier–client relationships has been receiving attention for some time, both in the general management literature and in operations management research.

The quality of the relationship will also depend on the quality of information sharing and the attitudes and dispositions as well as the social climate within which relationships are pursued.

It is the balance between relationship requirements and relationship capabilities that promotes the growth of outsourced arrangements. While it is critical to find the supplier/partner with the same values and principles in order to build a healthy outsourcing relationship, it is more critical to understand how suppliers deliver 'better' than the organizations they serve.

Ignorance and a lack of collaborative experience often take the blame as the main source of alliance problems and failures. This carries a unique risk in the ITO relationship. The transparency of the organization and the information available between partners can be achieved through active means, including the adopting of policies that enhance information sharing, or the deployment of shielding mechanisms in order to protect key competencies. This leads also to the point that complete integration is often neglected because of political or selfish reasons.

Outsourcing has evolved from spot-contracting to relationships where service providers offer products and services that advance the organization's strategic business goals and enhance the provider organization's position in the value chain. Organizations are observed to resort to consortia-based sourcing, namely, sourced service consortia, for the purposes of outsourcing key functions, particularly the IT function. Organizations are choosing from niche and speciality shops such as ASPs, Web hosting, and e-commerce providers, as well as network integration experts.

Suppliers of outsourcing services deliver products and services more efficiently than the buyers of these products and services. This is a fundamental assumption that forms the basis of the value gained in an outsourcing arrangement by the buyer of these services. The ability to 'buy' cost savings and efficiencies (in addition to many other things) from the supplier is the central benefit of outsourcing. However, a reduction in financial risks does not mean that the operational risks also diminish. It is this special relationship between the risk categories that becomes the central theme in Section II of this book.

The incentives for outsourcing suppliers are the increased margins and competitive advantage over competing supplier organizations. The need to perform at higher standards in terms of speed (volume output), cost of work done (cost of production) and quality of products/service delivery means that the supplier must innovate and perform better than the organization or buyer of these services. The risks of innovation must be considered by the supplier. What are the effects of this on the buyer's risk profile?

A supplier of services needs to cater to the needs of the buyer. The buyer of outsourcing services clearly seeks to derive maximum value directly through the outsourcing services and the positive effects the services would create in the various parts of the organization. While the supplier has profit motives, it seeks also to provide increased value to the buyer. It is demonstrated, however, that the value, in terms of goals and risk carried by the buyer and supplier, do not match. This produces a tension that is neither conducive to either group nor to the ideals originally designed to be delivered by strategic outsourcing. The risk profiles of both the buyer and supplier obviously change.

A further development has been that leading corporations acknowledge that the top tier of outsourcing organizations cannot be 'the best' in all areas, and hence have been contracting with two and/or a network of suppliers who are expected to co-operate in order to deliver a seamless service on behalf of their clients. Environmental and organizational risks are considered in this scenario.

The objectives of a typical outsourcing arrangement can be contractually specified. Methods and processes are, however, difficult to incorporate if they are based on tacit knowledge. Tacit knowledge is the result of an accumulation of experience and, as such, may be difficult to communicate to those without equivalent experience. Since contractors control work processes, unless they share the required tacit knowledge, they may choose suboptimal processes. Addressing this limitation may require intense day-to-day involvement of the organization's managers with the HR contractor until the contractor acquires the requisite tacit knowledge. Inefficiencies are likely to result, however, because managers may lack specific authority to direct work processes of contractors. Thus, because many positive HR outcomes depend on tacit knowledge, organizations that believe they have achieved such outcomes with in-house HR management are less likely to rely on HR outsourcing.

1.12 Outsourcing contracts

Effective contracting reduces the probability of many potential sources of loss. This serves to control legal risks. Unanticipated environmental changes create unanticipated opportunities for exploitation that were not protected against in the outsourcing contract. The probability of losses from residual risks is also determined by the unquantified probability that outsourcing partners will see and exploit these opportunities.

Contractual and/or informal relationships between the supplier and buyer organizations of these services are often structured around the nature of the outsourcing contracts and the use of market opportunities for competitive advantage. The various attributes of outsourcing contracts in the different types of outsourcing agreement vary. Outsourcing uses contractual mechanisms to help manage unique requirements and closely interlinked processes.

There are significant differences between the attributes of a sourcing contract and those of an outsourcing contract. However, various features encompass the contract mechanisms for both these concepts. When the price of the services is considered, often there are no 'market rates' for long-term contracts, especially with ITO, but often a negotiation process takes place. In an outsourcing deal, this is structured into a contract where possible formulae form the basis for pricing. In an outsourcing arrangement (versus a sourcing deal), the supplier typically is given a contract covering a long period of time (possibly 5 to 10 years) to deliver agreed outcomes over this period. In this instance there are high switching costs for both the buyer and supplier.

The services in a sourcing contract are tightly linked with the contract. When services are sourced (or purchased), the supplier provides the innovation, service and price at the time of purchase. In an outsourcing deal, the buyer determines the strategy, price, and contracted services that are delivered by the supplier.

The governance structure protects both the buyer and supplier in a long-term contract and agreement. During the outsourcing agreement period, the governance process allows for communications and an escalation process to resolve conflict. In a sourcing process, a supplier can be selected at any time.

Contractual risks are a dominant factor in the outsourcing decision. The drivers of risk derive from information asymmetries before contracting, inability to monitor partners' actions accurately, and exogenous changes that allow one party to behave opportunistically.

Governance infrastructure that will be in place at the start of the outsourcing contract will ensure that contracts are administered and processes are in place. Service level agreements are put into place. Service levels will be defined by the business functions and avoid highly technical metrics, as is well understood by business managers. The service levels also have clear and agreed consequences associated with failure to meet minimum standards.

The governance process ensures that the early agreements between the parties are adhered to. Finally, the customer's changing requirements are administered during the term of the contract, through the governance framework. This ensures appropriate arbitration as the supplier is often reluctant to change the contract without concessions or price increases. It also protects the supplier from unreasonable changes by the buyer.

The following are some supporting contract-related issues and related risks as observed by various experts. Despite the need for a clear contract, it is important that both the buyer and supplier must be ready to modify their means and ends as the outsourcing relationship develops. Not all aspects of the contract are foreseeable. A lengthy legal contract is not sufficient to manage this risk and protect what can be billions of dollars invested over an extended period of time. As retrospective documents that impose penalties after the fact, contracts are not suitable tools for remedying customer satisfaction. The outsourcing process is more effectively controlled through requirements definitions and formal change management systems.

The risks associated with the relationships form a key characteristic of the outsourcing agreement. Contractual difficulties can be grouped into a number of areas, involving precontract information asymmetries of supplier quality, inability to observe counterparty action, and opportunistic behaviour enabled by the bilateral relationship in an environment of great uncertainty and biases against comprehensive risk analysis.

An outsourcing contract between two parties is dictated by an enforceable contract. 'Contracts' can take a variety of forms ranging from a spot market contract where the terms are established and immediately satisfied after entering the agreement (for example, to buy or sell an existing mainframe to a predetermined deadline), to a long-term relational contract which simply agrees on a set of rules for future conduct without being explicit about everything each party is to do in every contingency. The critical limitation of contract structure, whatever the form, is that contract terms need to be enforceable. This requires a higher threshold than merely being observable by a third party. Contractual terms must also pass the more rigorous condition that they are verifiable to an outside party such as a court. There are a number of factors that influence the choice of governance structure. The ability to observe, monitor and verify the activities of both parties places restrictions on how detailed and effective an explicit contract can be.

1.13 Outsourcing and the implications for human resource development

Research shows that the success of outsourcing is more likely to be restrained by human rather than technological problems. In almost every situation where outsourcing is implemented, there is a reduction in the need for people. This often means that personnel are reassigned to another job function or are no longer needed in any capacity. These changes therefore often involve reductions in personnel in order to improve the efficiency of the organization in terms of cost disciplines and to maintain competitiveness in the market. The resultant organizational setup thus has both positive and negative consequences. Conversely, an ageing IT workforce is a factor for consideration in more mature markets (e.g. in North America) where retirements outpace the ability of governments to staff important technical functional areas.

Organizational performance can improve in three areas through the introduction of new skills and working practices, by reducing staff numbers, and by modifying individual incentives, employment terms and attitudes in the workplace. As management is more able to predict future costs than to predict future revenues, reducing costs by decreasing the size of the workforce is often done. Hence, the expected economic benefits of a smaller workforce include reduced expenses, increased returns on investment, higher profits and improved stock prices. Changes like these are often very emotive, generating internal fears as well as employee resistance.

Overall, it is acknowledged that whether the need for change in the organization is a consequence of a re-engineering of business processes and/or a focus on core competencies, or an attempt to restructure in order to become more globally competitive, and whether restructuring or outsourcing strategies are utilized, the resultant effect is downsizing. Redundancies and layoffs are commonplace in outsourcing situations despite the transfer of personnel to service providers, the redeployment of staff within the organization, outplacements and voluntary early retirements.

In the long term, the service provider relies more on natural attrition and redeployment as a means of aligning manpower to the contract. Even the transfer arrangements may have an impact on employment within the organization: on wages, on working conditions and on the duration of the contract with the new employer. Employees hence may perceive the prospect of outsourcing as tantamount to a sell-off, often along with capital equipment. Although many employees understand economic reality, i.e. that outsourcing efforts are undertaken for the improvement of organizational efficiency and to increase value to shareholders, questions are increasingly being asked concerning the emphasis on shareholder well-being to the detriment of stakeholders in the organization, namely employees. Effectively, employee loyalty to the organization diminishes in such circumstances.

Poaching, for example, is the misuse of information by another organization that has a close working relationship. Poaching occurs as, unlike the case with a physical asset, information is not subject to wear and tear and cannot be returned in the same way when it has finished being used. This enables organizations to appropriate information without obvious indications as to its use. This constitutes a subset of environmental or organizational risk. Organizational risk results from changes to internal organizational structures that occur as a result of changing roles. This risk will be reduced as organizations become more flexible, depending less on formal and rigid organizational structures.

The next chapter continues with a definition and description of risks that occur in the ITO environment. Risks, together with outsourcing activity and the unique nature of the IT function form the basis of first measuring, then understanding and subsequently mitigating, risks through planned activities in this high-profile environment.

2

Outsourcing the IT function

Risk-taking is an integral and intrinsic part of
success or living a full life.
Malcolm S. Forbes (1919–1990), US publisher

The outsourcing of the IT function often means that the organization's information requirements become a joint responsibility of a third party and the original organization. What is the risk then, if either the supplier or the buyer does not provide its end of the agreement? If we postpone the response to this question, and take a more optimistic perspective instead, i.e. consider the scenario wherein both sides deliver to expectations, the true value of information that can be derived from the IT function will be seen to be optimized.

The use of information is very subjective and quite dependent on the user's ability to leverage further advantage. Information that is left idle is not worth anything. If information is well used, the tiniest amount of information that is leveraged can return very significant benefits. It is argued that the value of information is derived from its accuracy (reliability), its relevance and its timeliness. Phrases like 'information is power', 'insider information' and 'business intelligence' represent attempts to describe the critical nature of information in many different scenarios to gain ascendancy and advantage. When the supplier can provide improved services from the IT function, the benefits to the buyer organization are certainly better than they were before.

Given the unique nature of each buyer/supplier encounter defined in the previous chapter, each ITO project is distinctive. In addition, the risks that become manifest are only applicable to the project at selected points in time. In the previous chapter, common concepts were referred to in the outsourcing environment. In this chapter, a baseline understanding of commonly used outsourcing frameworks is vital if the risks are to be measured from this common baseline. Each of these unique concepts contains inherent risks that influence the project. These risks need to be managed. The key concepts for illustration include the following:

- Core competency.
- Economies of scale and scope.
- Commoditization of the IT components (within the function).
- The dual role of IT within the organization.

The nature of IT not only refers to the equipment and related components but the nature and value of information. As a result, IT processes can be delegated but this also carries a level of risk that varies between organizations. It is difficult enough to identify the risk types let alone to quantify risk exposure in this environment. In an outsourced environment further questions need to be asked and answered. What, for example, are the capabilities/competencies of the parties involved with the delivery of the product that could introduce key operational risks? What are the delivery outcomes that determine a successful ITO agenda? How does the product contribute to a successful outcome for the buyer and/or the seller?

Many of the services offered to support the ubiquitous IT function are now commoditized. There is little differentiation in common processes, technology and capabilities. Over time, many common IT functions such as the maintenance and supply of routine software applications become commodity items that can be purchased as if they were mass produced. The organization's ability to maintain an IT function internally (within its own range of functions) has been used to provide a source of advantage; few organizations adopted the use of IT in their portfolio of capabilities only a decade ago. This is now no longer the case. For example, an organization may have a critical data warehouse function that provides information on its customers throughout the world. As storage was expensive in the late 1980s, its competitors could not afford to maintain large databases. And it was uncommon for an organization to be able to maintain a large data warehouse at that time. However, the situation has changed. Data storage has increased in quality and at the same time has undergone a very significant price reduction. Data storage services are now being charged on a cost-per-megabyte-per-month basis, similar to the way in which we all pay for utilities such as electricity and water. The commoditization of the data warehousing function has made data storage a commodity (as opposed merely to a feature that differentiates an organization that has data storage facilities).

As the existence of an IT function, at a generic level, loses its differentiated advantage relative to its competitors, IT service providers are more likely to increase their reliance on external suppliers and redirect their own capabilities to other high value-added areas. This argument supports outsourcing of the IT function. At the same time, however, it increases the level of competition among suppliers, who now need to seek ways to differentiate a generic service. Supplier organizations now need to maintain relevant skills, experience and capabilities to be able to deliver world-class IT services. The suppliers have the ability to deliver IT at a much lower cost and of significantly better quality than can other organizations without IT as their core competence.

2.1 The 'core competency' argument

Many organizations use outsourcing in the belief that ITO is a tool that provides the solution for lowering costs, improving service levels, accessing specialized resources and ensuring the success of new business ventures. The justification for the value provided by outsourcing the IT function is also made on the basis of the core competency argument. It has even been proposed by practitioners and researchers in this area that ITO should be an integral part of the organization's overall plan in order to focus on its core competence (Quinn and Hilmer, 1994; Venkatraman, 1997; DiRomualdo and Gurbaxani, 1998). Specifically, the organization needs to determine the scope of its activities with specific reference to its objectives, as opposed to outsourcing when there is a pressing need to apply cost disciplines.

The organization's corporate resources (personnel, computing equipment and other components) will be available to channel energies into the organization's core business or core competency.

The key components of core competence as defined by Prahalad and Hamel (1990) include:

- accessing a wide variety of markets;
- making a significant contribution to the perceived customer benefits of the end product; and
- making it difficult for competitors to imitate.

The focus on an organization's competency allows for resources to be maximized. Core competencies are like a bundle of corporate skills that cut across traditional functions, such as product or service design, technology creation, customer service and logistics. It is also suggested that core competencies can be regarded as distinctive competencies with multiple applications.

ITO satisfies cost reduction and enhancement of efficiency. Both the buyer and supplier organizations which are able to focus on core competence will more efficiently utilize resources and, hence, also deliver more cost-effective services. Resource-based organizational theory focuses on organizational business performance that makes efficient use of unique organizational capabilities supporting the creation of sustained performance within industries. Management ideas that stress the importance of downsizing of organizations also focus on key major activities to explain successful corporate performance (Hoskisson *et al.*, 1994).

In the outsourcing context, Alexander and Young (1996) describe core competency as tasks that are traditionally performed in-house; that are critical to business performance; that create current or potential competitive advantage; and that will drive further growth, innovation, or rejuvenation. This definition implies that core activities cannot be relinquished to a third party such as in an outsourcing situation. The question, however, whether IT is a core activity (and hence whether it should be outsourced) cannot be answered in a generalized sense. Core competencies are not seen as being fixed and codified but flexible and evolving over time. As the organization evolves and adapts to new circumstances and opportunities, so its core competencies will also adapt and change. In this way the organization will be able to make the most of its given resources and apply them to new opportunities.

Core competencies are those capabilities that are critical to an organization in its aim to achieve competitive advantage. A competence which is central to the organization's operations but which is not exceptional in some way should not be considered as a core competence, as it will not enable differentiation of the business from another similar type of business. For example, a process which requires the use of common computer components and is staffed by people with only basic training cannot be regarded as a core competence. Such a process is highly unlikely to generate a differentiated advantage over rival businesses. However, it is possible to develop such a process such that it becomes a core competence with suitable investment in equipment and training.

Performance of the IT function

A plethora of tools and techniques are available which can measure the performance of competing IT strategies and investments in processes including the outsourcing of the IT function. In addition to metrics like returns on investment (ROI), internal rate of return (IRR) and net present value (NPV), an IT function of an organization must also meet certain fundamental performance criteria including reliability, availability, security and manageability.

Core competencies are a mix of technological specialization, innovative input, and the degree of diversification or specialization of organizational resources (Markides and Williamson, 1994). Following this argument, core competence suggests the ability of an organization to provide excellent performance, over and above normal standards. Additionally, core competencies include a pool of experience, knowledge, and systems developed by the organization that, together, can be used to create and accumulate new strategic assets. The focus on the importance of understanding the performance of the organization is a result of the efficient use of these distinct capabilities that create sustained performance and competitive advantage.

While the supplier focuses on its core competence in delivering the IT functions, the buyer enjoys relief from not having to focus on non-core competence activities. As both organizations focus on individual core competence or activities (specialization), efficiencies are gained. The view from the literature is that service quality improvement, the need for strategic flexibility and the focus on core competencies are predominant concerns for sourcing decisions. Outsource activity improves operations within the organization through focus on core competence.

The major drivers for outsourcing, however, include cost-effective access to specialized skills provided by the new commercial arrangement. Indirect overhead costs or 'non-core competencies' are outsourced to achieve cost-effective operations through economies of scale. Cumulative experience in outsourcing enhances quality improvement, with concomitant cost reduction.

Organizations are now focusing on 'core' business in the search for greater efficiency. This effort to focus on core products has also had the effect of reducing costs and exploiting new channels of distribution, such as the Internet.

If these claims were to be viewed from a more pragmatic perspective, then having a competence alone does not, on its own, guarantee success. Competitive advantage depends on whether the competence helps deliver a product or service that customers value. It is a differentiation of products/services that gives the organization its advantage and also allows premium pricing of its services.

Advantages gained by using outsourcing services are derived from cost leadership and access to lower overheads, and differentiation through access to new technology and a supply of more competent people. As outsourced services are no longer managed within the organization, it follows that its services are most effective in a highly networked environment where information flows unhindered. Further, operational efficiencies are derived as organizations focus on core competence or main activities. Many non-core activities are reassigned or allocated to another party in an outsourcing arrangement. This enables the buyer organization to apply more attention, effort and resources to activities that contribute directly to its business. It is argued that the organization's ability to make the decision either to have a capability to deliver the IT function or to use an external supplier is, in essence, its core competency.

Distinctive competency

When the core competence of an organization is sufficiently different or distinctive from those which other organizations possess, it allows that organization to command the market in terms of product price; this means that it has a control advantage. This difference or distinctive competency, in turn, allows the organization to earn a return above marginal costs plus cost of capital. IT supports unique processes and the specialist role thereof reinforces this situation.

One of the arguments used to assess the level of technological specialization of an organization lies in the use of patent statistics. The concentration of patents indicates choices with regard to priority skills and concentrated innovative capabilities. Patents have been, arguably, an acceptable indicator of research output and technological competence. Patents could serve as an indicator of whether an organization has been able to turn its research and other innovative activities into inventions that are worth protecting. For the purposes of this argument however, many IT functions could then be patented.

This discussion on the usefulness of patents, however, has relevance to our argument as it does generally show that a competence is worth protecting. The patenting of IT processes is, however, rare as a result of the speed of change and rapid growth in the industry. This does not allow for the possibility that there may be several organizations with above-average competencies in an industry constituted by a large number of organizations. Since, therefore, a particular competence is not unique, it is unlikely to attract a premium pricing strategy. The IT function hence is a mix of new ideas and knowledge as well as proven and used concepts. Following this argument, each part of the function should be investigated thoroughly in an outsourcing exercise. The next argument, however, indicates otherwise.

Assuming there is a set of distinctive competencies within an organization's IT function, many would argue that the cumulative and tacit nature of technological knowledge in the IT function is very difficult to transfer from one organization to another. In an outsourcing situation, the identifiable elements of distinctive advantage can in any case be restricted via isolated scope of work, contracts and other instruments. So, more importantly, the intellectual property risks involved in an outsourcing exercise should be investigated.

Diversification and specialization

The degree of diversification is relevant for understanding the role of core competencies to the extent that it affects the performance of the organization. From a supplier perspective, the benefits of specialization are essential to deliver better service. From the buyer perspective an outsourcing exercise enhances the degree of specialization. Both parties benefit from the outsourcing exercise. The degree of relatedness of lines of business, which comes closer to specialization in the light of core capabilities, is hence observed to be positively related to the economic performance of diversified organizations. This supports the outsourcing-of-IT argument that organizations should become focused and specialized.

There is, however, another view that the diversification of organizations increases economic performance through risk mitigation. It is difficult to establish a positive relationship between the degree of diversification of organizations and their profitability. In fact, there are many examples that indicate that the degree of organizations' diversification is related negatively to their economic performance. Whether diversification or specialization, the risks involve relate directly to the ability of each party to benefit from the advantages inherent in these concepts. How then are the risks going to be measured and quantified in order to negotiate the best terms for either the buyer or supplier?

Outsourcing to derive the benefits of core competency

Outsourcing allows a key function like IT to be effectively removed (resources, assets and operations) while the organization still 'enjoys' the selected outcomes from this function (use of IT to enable the flow of information within the organization). Non-core functions therefore can be effectively removed as regular operations are passed to the supplier of outsourcing services who, in turn, will deliver the desired outcomes to the buyer of these services. When organizations focus on core competence, advantages of economies of scale, cost reduction and more-effective operations often result. Among organizations that have outsourcing agreements, satisfaction is higher for those that out-source core activities, provided that they incur minimal risk from the relationship established.

Organizations should define the areas critical to their success, devote maximum resources to those areas, and outsource every-thing else that is not 'core'. As defined earlier, the competencies of the organization provide potential access to a wide variety of markets, make a significant contribution to the perceived cus-tomer benefits of the end product, and are difficult for competi-tors to imitate. A definition of core competence includes activities that the organization is continuously engaged in, while periph-eral activities are those that are intermittent and, therefore, can be outsourced. If this strategic perspective is adopted, the argu-ment then holds that core activities should stay in-house, while non-core activities can be outsourced, in order to preserve core competencies. The importance of coherence in corporate cap-abilities that strengthen the competitive advantages of organiza-tions needs to be emphasized. Multi-business organizations with commonalities based on shared capabilities and know-how are known to be associated with higher economic perform-ance (Prahalad and Hamel, 1990).

To cope with increasingly aggressive environmental pressures, organizations are attempting to reposition themselves higher on the value chain so as to gain competitive advantage. In an effort to transform cost-based activities into profit centres, some organizations use separately managed profit centres or business units to induce competitive market pressures internally. These supplementary or non-core activities are then spun off into sep-arate organizations with the intent of making them profitable. This, however, appears to be a solution for situations where there is logical placement of these functions within the organization.

For example, organizations that supply outsourcing services for profit motives leverage on economies of scale to provide cost-effective and resource-efficient services. The 'economies of scale' argument is discussed below.

2.2 The 'economies of scale' argument

Another common reason why organizations choose to outsource is to achieve economies of scale. Both the buyer and supplier of the ITO function would benefit from the effects of economies of scale and scope.

Outsourcing has moved markedly from attending to a single function more efficiently, to reconfiguring a whole process in order to achieve greater shareholder value across the organization. The emphasis is shifting from outsourcing parts, facilities and components, towards outsourcing the intellectually based systems, such as customer response handling, procurement and management. Herein are the benefits that can be obtained through economies of scale and scope. Equally, however, the perceived risks are greater.

When a buyer has contracted for IT services, it has assured itself a portion of any profit that would be received from selling excess capacity on its systems. If the supplier could use the additional capacity to serve other buyers, economies of scale are realized. Large suppliers also have the scale to negotiate better acquisition terms for software and hardware. By purchasing in larger quantities to serve simultaneous users, suppliers can lower per-unit costs. Finally, software developed for a specific application can often be applied at virtually no incremental cost to other clients. For this reason many large third-party suppliers appear in markets where a service is principally delivered through software.

The effects of economies of scale are significant. For example, a software developer would incur a one-time cost in the development of a software application. Each copy sold subsequently would earn a unit cost. Each unit sold would then contribute to a share of the original capital costs. The outsourced supplier, however, would purchase one licence to run the application at a unit cost. Subsequently this supplier would 'host' the application for multiple buyers. Software suppliers have since, however, changed this procedure by licensing software not by machine, but by 'concurrent users' or 'seats'. This example illustrates some of the magnification effects of scale economies that exist in an outsourcing environment.

Economies of scale have their limits in an ITO context and are only verified for the cost of machine or CPU time and not services. For example, a supplier would need a finite number of people to support a particular function. People resources are finite and cannot be broken down into partial resources. Perfect economies of scale hence do not occur in all aspects of economies of scale. People costs dominate in governance and service costs; both of which can be unpredictable as they would only be required when there is a need. The financial and resource risks that are incurred by the supplier need to be accounted for here. Likewise the same risks are passed on to the buyer if not adequately taken up by the supplier.

Economies of scale can also be observed when network externalities affect the organization's decisions in a situation where a product or service becomes more valuable to all users, as its adoption grows. For example, the 'Voice Over Internet Protocol' (VoIP) system is of little use if only one person has access to the network, whereas it has an enormous value if a person from the organization can call virtually anyone for a low charge. Products, services or systems that exhibit network externalities tend to converge toward standards. Once a standard has attained critical mass, organizations may recognize that adhering to the standard is critical for survival as economies are realized.

The main advantage the supplier organizations have lies in economies of scale and scope. The benefits from economies of scale arise when costs decline as production increases. The most common form of an economy of scale is when efficient production involves a large fixed cost, such as the initial capital outlay to procure some of the buyer organization's assets, amortized via a larger quantity of goods or services. Increasingly, outsourcing suppliers are now looking beyond running IT systems to business process management (BPM), in which they also take over functions such as billing, cheque processing and accounting.

The benefits of economies of scope, much like the economies of scale, are enjoyed by the supplier where shared fixed-cost equipment for multiple buyer organizations can be pooled and used for a common core of IT services. Generally the supplier will negotiate for activities where the total costs of delivering a common portion of the IT function lie across several buyer organizations (in a sharing scheme). These costs will be lower than the sum of the costs of producing them separately, hence the benefit from economies of scope. An example of economies of scope is when core technologies have applications across multiple industries. A detailed study of 186 systems projects between the years 1967 and 1993 in five large organizations which implemented new technologies such as fourth-generation programming languages, or which required mini-computers or multiple-computer networks, found that they were more likely to be outsourced than built in-house (Nelson *et al.*, 1996). Rapid technological change, combined with the experience of working in different settings, often gives suppliers the advantage in providing 'leading edge' technology services.

2.3 Commoditization of IT

Many of the discussions around core competency no longer apply when IT becomes a commodity item. The use of IT components has become prolific and their availability abundant. There is little restriction on access to outsourced services and products. Easy access, over time, would result in standardized (mass production, repeat transaction) outsourced services. The differentiation which used to exist with respect to lower cost, resource availability and access to expertise has become diluted. The standardized processes which used to be outsourced now serve as building blocks or a foundation for a more complex series of interrelationships and risk elements.

2.4 The role of IT in the organization

The IT function is typically used to perform infrastructure support but it can also be utilized to differentiate an organization's products and services.

It is a support function as it is interwoven or integrated into many essential organizational processes and is an essential tool that enables many value-creation activities to go ahead. The IT function itself, however, can take on several roles in an organization including that of a strategic function which allows the organization to differentiate itself from its competitors, i.e. as a primary function. This 'dual function and capability' feature of IT adds another dimension of complication to the outsourcing decision, as this function is unsuitable for being outsourced in specific situations, i.e. when it is a strategic function that differentiates the organization from its competitors. The organization retains control of the strategic function to protect itself against possible theft – or other criminal activity (by a competitor) – of its proprietary information. The operational risk as well as risk of loss of information is higher in this situation.

For example, when an organization's IT application is used to enable the establishment of a specialized e-commerce channel that its competitors do not possess, it becomes a strategic function for this organization. In another similar organization in another country or business setting, the same IT application may be used by most of the other members of the organization's industrial sector. In this setting, it is commoditized and has the role of a support function. The risk profile involved, when a strategic role applies, may be different when compared to the supporting role scenario.

There are many options available to mitigate the risk of information loss and operational downtime as well as erosion of technical and business advantage. A mechanism to reduce these risks has traditionally been a legal document called the buyer–supplier agreement. As this new tier of risks is introduced, the magnitude of risk exposure applying to the legal and operational risk groups increases. It is this fluctuation in risk for each of the risk groups that will be investigated in this book.

The role IT plays in the organization determines the strategy and route taken when it is outsourced. After the decision to outsource is made, however, the relevance (of its role) diminishes. The success of the outcomes of an IT service then comes to the forefront.

2.5 Outsourcing and the unique role(s) of the IT function

As a strategic or primary function, IT networks encourage vertical de-integration of organizations by lowering the costs of 'buying' compared to 'making' in-house. Reduced co-ordination costs imply an 'unbundling' of functions, making it easier and more efficient to enter into value chains rather than maintain in-house ownership. This provides opportunities for the IT function, which has a role as a competitive weapon for the organization. When IT as a supporting function is outsourced, there are obvious benefits to be gained. When IT is a primary function, however, the competitive advantage is enhanced through the strengths of the organization of origin in partnership with the supplier. The successful performance of the IT function hence, no longer pertains to the outsourcing organization but to the supplier that has been selected for its superior delivery of IT outcomes. The ability to provide both a support as well as a strategic role within the organization is unique to the IT function. In both these roles, separate outsourcing models are used.

As the role of IT changes, the outsourcing decision and governance tactics change. To illustrate this, Figures 2.1 and 2.2 show some of the possible choices. In Figure 2.1, the IT function is shown as a primary (strategic) function and as a support function on the x-axis. The organization's position, i.e. whether the IT function is outsourced or not, is indicated on the y-axis. As IT can be a strategic or primary function within an organization, outsourcing is seldom optimal (marked with an 'X'). When IT is used as a competitive weapon, it should not be outsourced under most circumstances. This is because the risks of losing information and the competitive advantage from the differential created is lost if the supplier 'leaks' or shares this information with competitors of the buyer organization.

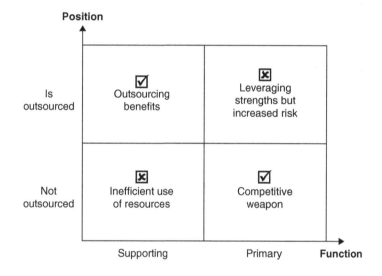

Figure 2.1
The role of IT and its position in the organization value chain (Tho, 2002)

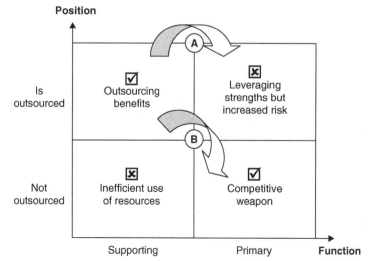

Figure 2.2
In the transition from support to primary function, path A involves high risk if the supplier–buyer relationship is not managed, and path B is optimal (Tho, 2002)

In the case where IT is a supporting function, shown in the left-hand quadrants in Figure 2.1, a decision to keep the supporting function internal often results in inefficient use of resources, loss of focus and unnecessary costs. A decision not to outsource in this situation is often 'suboptimal'. Optimal outsourcing benefits are realized when supporting functions are outsourced.

In an environment where the outsourced IT function changes from a support to a primary (strategic) role within the organization, the decision to continue to outsource is based very much on the risk exposure in the operational, business and strategic areas, which influence the decision. The decision to maintain the strategy to outsource and the risks associated with this now need to be considered (path A or path B in Figure 2.2). Path A would mean that the IT function continues to be outsourced. This will mean that the operational, business and other risks escalate because a third party has access to confidential and proprietary information. A decision to discontinue outsourcing, path B, may be selected if the 'appetite' of the organization for risk ('risk appetite') is exceeded. In this instance, the organization then decides to shift its IT function internally and to be managed using its internal resources.

Many instances have been cited where organizations which once had the IT function performing internal support functions have shifted this role to facilitate primary e-commerce operations; for example web channel marketing, purchasing online and supply chain management. A large group of IT functions have become standardized, or commoditized; these functions are prime candidates for outsourcing.

The imposition of unplanned, higher fees backed up by the supplier's threats to discontinue service or by other unmanageable threats, is frequently termed supplier hold-up. As a result of the complex characteristics of IT in the outsourcing situation, there is a high risk of exposure and a high probability of failure inherent in IT operations; this is in addition to the risks of the relationship between the supplier and buyer of outsourcing services also resulting in failure in this activity. There have been many warnings of organizations experiencing negative consequences of ITO activity including escalating costs, diminishing service levels, loss of expertise, and contract irreversibility.

Which activities should remain within the 'buyer' organization, in order to maximize the advantages of outsourcing? Unless the organization develops best-in-world capabilities, including transaction cost disciplines, it should purchase goods/services from providers who have best-in-world skills, in order to achieve a competitive edge. It has also been suggested that ' "core" means "keep" ', or that an organization's core activities should be kept within the organization and never allowed to be performed by a third party.

As a result of the cumulative and tacit nature of technological knowledge, which is of particular relevance in so-called high-tech industries, it is assumed that this kind of knowledge is often very difficult to transfer from one organization to another and therefore cannot be acquired easily through arm's-length transactions but only through very closely integrated networks.

The IT productivity paradox and outsourcing

There is a choice between carrying out activities in-house and placing them under market governance (via outsourcing), as determined by the relative costs of production and transactions. Not long ago, organizations were observed to have a voracious appetite for rapidly improving technology. Measured productivity gains were insignificant. Businesses have since been revolutionized, along with the way we work, with permanent change derived from the use of new technology, computers and related computer peripheral devices. Only a couple of decades ago, there was heated debate on the value of computers and computerization. Could it be argued that businesses are experiencing a similar phenomenon with the use of the familiar outsourcing services that now support the complete IT function? There were major success stories and equally many impressive failures in the use of IT only a decade ago, and there have been many case studies that indicate catastrophic consequences and failures in early ITO activity.

In a paper from research work at Harvard University, it was reported that most of the productivity slowdown was concentrated in the service sector. In the same paper it was argued that IT is an effectively used substitute for labour in most manufacturing industries, but has paradoxically been associated with bloating white-collar employment in services, especially finance. At the same time, it was indicated that the apparent paradox could be attributed to several basic causes. The reasons used included the inappropriate measurement of outputs and inputs, lags in the learning and adjustment cycle, redistribution and dissipation of profits, and mismanagement of information and technology. Possible errors in measurement and statistical or research error appear to be the main causes of the paradox. The mismanagement of information and technology begs the question whether managers have improperly managed and used IT. This is particularly relevant to the outsourcing of the IT function as observations of the current literature on ITO seem to mirror these arguments.

There are many examples of mismanagement and misappropriation of resources and activities in the IT function. There is also the point regarding hidden costs, which is glaringly obvious and high-profile.

Hidden costs

Costs are difficult to measure and quantify for a particular exercise in a typical organization. As outsourcing leads to a redefinition of organizational boundaries and, by implication, structural adjustments involving human resources, these changes often result in social as well as financial costs. Although these costs are not permanent and are mitigated through retraining and redeployment of people resources within the organization, their transfer to the supplier organization can result in considerable redundancy payouts. The costs of outsourcing are not uniformly distributed among the stakeholders of the organization and the effects of contracting out on overall employment levels in the economy are not well researched or understood.

The costs of outsourcing are composed of the costs of carrying out the transaction and, in addition, hidden costs due to co-ordination difficulties and contractual risks. These hidden costs have often not been accounted for in the outsourcing exercise. This is as a result of the relative inexperience of buyers seeking to use outsourcing services. Unlike suppliers, buyers do not have the benefit of past experience. The savings gained as a result of economies of scale are then theoretically translated as direct savings for the tasks outsourced by the buyer. Sometimes other costs that are incurred as a result of implementing the outsourcing framework offset these savings. For example, the costs of becoming dependent on outside suppliers for services can destroy all the benefits of outsourcing. When control is lost over a critical function like IT and faced with the prospect of managing relationships that go wrong and lowering the morale of permanent employees, the move towards outsourcing becomes a significant hidden cost to outsourcing. This eventuality forms the biggest risk to the buyer, and is seen to outweigh many of the other benefits. It is an element of risk, i.e. an event that is driven by a low probability and that therefore may not happen. Outsourcing can also generate other new risks for the buyer, such as the loss of critical skills or developing the wrong skills, the loss of cross-functional skills, and the loss of control over suppliers. These risks are especially pertinent when the supplier's priorities do not match buyer needs.

For the organization that buys outsourcing services, outsourcing activity provides it with the ability to adjust the scale and scope of its production capability upwards or downwards, at a lower cost, to meet changing demand conditions. In addition, outsourcing decreases the product/process design cycle time. With the use of multiple best-in-class suppliers, who work simultaneously on individual components of the system, each supplier contributes greater depth and sophisticated knowledge in specialized areas and thus offers higher-quality inputs than can any individual supplier or client. The cost margins that previously existed when the IT function was performed in-house no longer exist as the services from the supplier would either cost the same or less than when the IT function was performed internally.

Buyers often have no basis or ability to budget for costs of contracting for services involving searching for a suitable supplier, negotiating a fair price, writing the contract, monitoring performance and enforcing the contract. Other costs include co-ordination among the different organizations, bridging cultural gaps among participants, and risks inherent in contractual relations. Contractual risks pose probably the largest transaction cost in procuring IT services. These benefits appear to be greater than the costs of monitoring that arise from supervision and legal arrangements.

Transferring fixed costs into variable costs by selling assets to an outsourcing supplier is also considered an advantage for many organizations. An organization receives a cash payment and transfers fixed costs into variable overheads. These overheads are adjusted in line with increases and decreases in business. This is beneficial in the majority of businesses.

With outsourcing there is a balance between the costs of running a larger, less specialized organization and the costs that arise from search issues and imperfect contracting. An organization that decides to outsource its IT components must search for a suitable partner, and then try to provide this partner with incentives to produce service inputs to its specifications and to the timeliness of the information it demands. Searching is costly and does not always end in success. When an organization decides to maintain its IT function (along with others), however, it faces higher costs of producing components and services, because of the many divisions left to manage, and because it cannot benefit from the learning and expertise that is acquired with specialization in a single activity.

Financial accounting methods of product costing, aimed mainly at profit calculation for the whole organization, do not usually provide complete and relevant information of this sort. Hidden costs come simply from choosing the relevant time period for comparing own and supplier costs/prices, and choosing the scope of own and supplier costs/prices for comparison. In addition, the most important decision variables are usually not quantified (e.g. safeguarding own know-how, maintaining hi-tech image).

2.6 Information technology outsourcing risk

Risk is a common feature with any business endeavour. As ITO is like any other business activity, risks are an integral part of the ITO exercise. Unlike most business environments, however, ITO involves a very long term relationship with a supplier of outsourcing services. This also means that there is a wide range of risks for ITO that need to reflect the dynamics of the arrangement, the fast-paced IT industry and changes in people including leadership, workers and customers. The risks (previously identified as pure risks) occurring in an ITO exercise are unique and relate specifically to (1) the IT function itself (comprising operations and development of components), and (2) the ITO deal.

ITO arrangements represent promises between a buyer and supplier of IT services over an agreed period. Along with this are the associated contract risks over the same period. A contractual agreement that benefits both the buyer and supplier of ITO services, therefore, naturally also contributes to a successful outsourcing relationship. An essential component of this outsourcing relationship is the governance of the ITO exercise. Inherent in the governance activities are changes that need to be agreed and subsequently made in the contract or agreement between the parties. As result of inevitable influences from the dynamic business and operating environment, changes need to be reflected in the contracts. This governance process will ensure that both parties continue to share maximum benefits and also an equitable portion of the risks that manifest in the ITO exercise.

In addition to a consideration of risks of contract amendments and disputes leading to litigation, an increased understanding of the different types of risks encountered by each of the contracting parties would allow for more effective governance of contracts, which mitigates the risks and balances difficulties between the parties.

Before the risks in an ITO are discussed in detail, it is necessary to establish a common understanding of several key concepts in an ITO exercise. The most common of the concepts misunderstood is the 'core competency' argument and the risk elements that are carried along with the use of this notion.

The IT function has a unique role in any organization, especially in the current economy. It is different from any other function within the organization. When it is outsourced special consideration needs to be given to it.

Many managers, IT practitioners and researchers in this area warn of risks when embarking on the outsourcing of the organization's IT function. Part of the reason for this is because there are very few data available on the organizations' risk tolerance (or ability to absorb the effects of risk) when embarking on an ITO exercise. The innate inability to understand and subsequently manage the risks involved is a factor that contributes significantly to this hesitance. There is scant knowledge on the effects of actions to mitigate risk exposure in an ITO exercise. Little wonder, then, why many organizations remain reluctant to outsource the IT function. It is often decided not to outsource the IT function at all, or to take only partial measures, in which case the benefits of outsourcing the IT function are often not fully realized.

We know from the work done in the area of outsourcing that one of the benefits accruing is the ability to move some of the operational risks encountered in the IT function from the buyer to the supplier organization. This ability to shift the risks to an organization that is more capable of managing the risks is valuable to the buyer organization. It allows the buyer organization to focus on other tasks and frees resources that would otherwise have to be allocated to managing the IT operations and associated risks.

The dominant sources of risk derive from information asymmetry (between buyer and supplier), the inherent inability to monitor the partner's actions, and exogenous changes that allow one party to behave opportunistically during the period of the partnership. It is, hence, a gargantuan task to understand the causes, effects and nature of all the risks that manifest in an ITO exercise. A selected portion of the risks in the ITO exercise is highlighted in this book to illustrate very specific risks that play a vital role in the decision to outsource the IT function. It is this nature and behaviour of key risk elements that needs to be addressed each time an organization outsources its IT function. The risk elements deliver opposing results or yields, i.e. being either constructive or destructive to the organizations that participate in the exercise.

It is known that a certain amount of risk shifts from the buyer to the supplier of outsourcing services. This is a phenomenon that is taken advantage of most in a typical ITO exercise and is seen as a benefit by the buyer of the services. The transfer of risks between buyer and supplier occurs almost as soon as the outsourcing exercise commences. As would be expected, operational risks are transferred away from the buyer organization as risks that accompany the IT operations. The supplier, on the other hand, takes on the new operations and associated risks as part of the agreement and is compensated through a service fee.

It is observed, however, that despite this obvious benefit, the buyer organization often hesitates to shift the IT operations outside the organization for fear that the loss of control may be unsustainable. The buyer is also often anxious over the uncertainty caused by a range of new risks that it has to manage as a result of the ITO exercise. The supplier, on the other hand, appears willingly to absorb the operational risks, which contributed to the reason why the buyer initiated the outsourcing exercise in the first place.

These traits provide a background to interesting insights into the management and nature of shifting risks both within and between the buyer and supplier organizations. The final chapter in this book highlights this phenomenon and includes an illustration of a set of observable traits that exist between risk groupings when the IT function of an organization is outsourced.

Managers in the same organizations that purchase the use of IT components argue that the in-house IT function not only comprises components that are often referred to as 'commodity' functions, but form an essential and strategic part of the overall corporate strategy. The IT function, in this instance, differentiates the organization's services and products from those of its competitors. The IT function is no longer a commodity but a strategic component. As such, the IT function contains 'secrets' that are often not shared, to preserve the competitive advantage.

The supplier of the IT function, however, has established a special relationship with the buyer organization. Confidentiality and security become very important as areas of high risk. This relationship is more than that of a casual supplier; rather, one where the integrity of the information and technology delivered becomes vital. It is often argued that, unlike manufacturing industry where products can be protected via legal instruments such as patents, information flows are more difficult to control. Fraudulent and criminal use of information is often difficult to trace or police; and therefore the risk of sharing one's information with a third party is often viewed as an unacceptable risk.

In both these instances (commodity versus strategic roles), however, it is still quite plausible and conceivable that the use of the concept of ITO along with its many variants, is able to deliver significant and tangible benefits to both the buyer and supplier organizations. The difference lies in the 'integrity and reliability' of the supplier as compared to an in-house maintained IT function. This difference is often observed as it becomes manifest in the risk exposure and risk profile of the buyer and supplier organizations. In this chapter, some of the fundamental ideas of outsourcing of the IT function have been discussed; they need to be understood in order to experience, identify and measure the risks that manifest themselves in this environment. For it is only when risks are quantified that they can also be mitigated in order to enjoy the maximum benefits of true IT outsourcing. This is discussed in Section II.

Section II

Measuring and understanding
IT outsourcing risks

3

Measuring risks in IT outsourcing

*Without measureless and perpetual uncertainty the drama of
human life would be destroyed.*
Winston Churchill (1874–1965), British prime minister

Risks in IT outsourcing (ITO) are often the effects of a combination of activities and events. These events can arise both at different times and in different geographical locations. For example, an event in the Head Office in Singapore last month could have very significant effects on another event in Sydney, Australia, today and affect another activity in San Francisco the following week. Various methods and tools are used to help measure and quantify these activities and events. The risk dimension signature (RDS) instrument proposed in this chapter allows measurements to be made from the various risk perspectives, and then graphically illustrates the risk exposure values (or measured quantities) at different points in time. The risk profiles that are depicted in the RDS then become an essential part of overall risk management methodology that allows the manager to understand risks more completely and make informed decisions. RDS transforms risk management from an academic or mathematical exercise into an essential and practical tool.

Risks involve events that are characterized by probability and uncertainty. They also stem from possibilities and indeterminate paths as a result of random events. We know that ITO is characterized by:

- multiple variations in outsourcing models (Chapter 1); and
- the two very special roles that the IT function plays in an organization (Chapter 2).

This, combined with the complexities of both the buyer and supplier organizations in a synergistic, long-term relationship, creates an environment that is full of events and 'risk fertile', or full of risks.

Measurement activity to capture these risks is more complex than ever before, partly as a result of the intricacies involved with available options and volumes of information flows that power today's fast-moving organizational processes. The probability of an event happening, whether with good or bad consequences, is never predictable to any degree of certainty. In fact, uncertainty in the economy, in technology, in business and in politics has made forecasting based on probabilities quite futile and, sometimes, even counter-productive.

In order to understand risks, however, detailed observation and measurement is mandatory. So the first step in the process is to be able to take measurements and to illustrate the results in a way that is meaningful to the ITO manager or practitioner. If the risk characteristics that are expressed in the specific ITO assignment can be measured, activities to mitigate the risks can be put into place for selected risks. A simplified step methodology involving three basic steps, Measure, Understand and Mitigate (MUM), as illustrated in Figure 3.1, is used to show the three fundamental phases that are used to address risks before a more comprehensive risk management method is used.

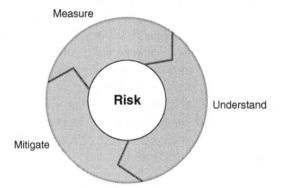

Figure 3.1
Managing risks in
an IT outsourcing
environment

Obviously a complete risk management methodology is comprehensive but the MUM method addresses the need to quickly depict and address urgent risks and allows plans to be effective as critical risks will need to be addressed urgently. Therefore more detailed risk management methods should be used in conjunction with the three phases proposed. This approach is designed to be short, and to be as practicable as possible for easy use. Given these assumptions, it should also be used in conjunction with organizational communications that include policy making, suitable controls and the promotion of risk awareness programmes (see also samples of widely accepted risk management models in Figures 3.5 and Figure 3.6). These items or activities form part of the overall risk management plan (see Chapter 6).

3.1 Risk definition

For simplicity, many scholars and researchers agree to define risk in an ITO scenario simply as **the possibility of loss or injury**. Risks begin as a direct consequence of negative outcomes. Risks are also formed as an extension of factors leading to negative outcomes. Risks refer either directly to:

- negative outcomes; or
- factors that lead to the negative outcomes.

Negative outcomes include shortfalls in systems performance. For example, in the case of a software development project, poor systems performance could take the form of disruption of service to a customer that depends on IT to support a particular business process function. In an ITO exercise, hidden costs (described in Chapter 2) and loss in innovative capacity would constitute examples of poor systems performance. Factors that lead to these negative outcomes include, for example, a continuing stream of requirement changes or personnel shortfalls in a systems development context. In an ITO project, lack of upper management commitment to the exercise or inexperienced staff and business uncertainty are clearly factors that lead to negative outcomes. The existence of vague links between the outcomes and contributory factors does not make the understanding of risks any easier or measurement more straightforward.

Risks can be quantified as expected potential loss. To do this, the expected potential loss from outsourcing is reckoned as the product of two variables, the magnitude of the exposure and the probability of loss.

3.2 Investigating risk

Risks are classified as either speculative or pure risks. Speculative risks (e.g. gambling) offer both the potential for gain and the potential for loss, for example in investment in stocks. Pure risks, the kind that occur in an ITO exercise, do not necessarily result in losses, but they never result in gains and are, for the most part, unwanted.

To reduce the loss or mitigate risks, efforts are focused on reducing the probability of the undesirable event itself through, for example, the use of penalties compensating for delays in system delivery. The probability of occurrence of an undesirable outcome is estimated on the basis of historical data. Probabilities are often, however, difficult to determine merely on the basis of past performance. In the case study example in Chapter 8, it is obvious that the probabilities estimated by the ITO team represent quantitative data based on collective experience.

Intrusive factors (exogenous and endogenous risks)

Further, a distinction that could be made in risk types is the classification of endogenous and exogenous risk. A risk is classified exogenous when an undesirable event occurs beyond any form of control and is not affected directly by any actions. Examples are earthquakes or typhoons. Endogenous risks are those that are dependent directly on people actions. An automobile accident is an example of risk where a large portion of the risk is endogenous. The probability of a virus attack is significantly influenced by the user's behaviour and software use (endogenous). The PC user controls part of this risk by deciding to expose corporate networks through unwanted links on the network. To mitigate this risk, users are informed of the areas they can control and are advised on more restrictive practices to adopt when surfing the Internet and performing downloads.

In a business environment, the dynamics of risk exposure can be, and are, influenced by many variables. The magnitude of these variables, in singular or group form, collectively determines their relevance. For example, the effects of risk on the finances of an organization can be influenced by its shareholder structure, the business environment (which determines the amount of investment), the technology environment (which determines the capability of performing selected functions) and the competitive environment (which determines its products, delivery and organizational structure). These factors 'intrude' into the outsourcing environment. It has been shown that these 'intrusive factors' contribute to the risk profile of the outsourced operation.

Risk dimensions are affected at different levels by external (exogenous) influences of 'intrusive factors' discussed earlier as well as internal (endogenous) influences. An example of the influences impinging on risk factors is illustrated in Figure 3.2. Environmental and business risk in the case study (see Chapter 8) for example, derives from external influences, discussed in detail here. The organization's strategic, legal and informational risk profiles are influenced most significantly by a mix of both internal and external influences.

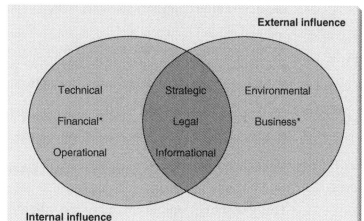

Figure 3.2
Example of
mapping internal
(endogenous) and
external (exogenous)
influences with risk
dimensions (Tho,
2004)

Operational and relationship risks

There are two main angles from which risk that is inherent in an
ITO arrangement is viewed. The first is the operational risk that
involves undesirable consequences deriving from the operations
of IT in the organization. The second form of risk stems from the
relationship between the buyer and supplier in the form of opportunistic behaviour by the supplier who takes advantage of a
long-term and ambiguous contract (see also Agency Theory in
Chapter 4). Both these risk types are illustrated in Figure 3.3.
A significant portion of the operational risk is passed on to the
supplier as the IT function is outsourced while the relationship
risk remains with the buyer. Unlike operations risk, the relationship risk is 'bi-directional'. In this instance, the risk exposure
relating to the relationship can be passed back and forth
depending on the situation and the 'bargaining power' of both
the contracting parties at that time. The relationship risk shifts
from buyer to supplier and vice versa.

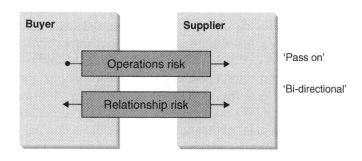

Figure 3.3
Operations and
relationship risk
(Tho, 2003)

Further relationship risk exposure from the outsourcing deal includes some common areas such as:

- misaligned incentives between supplier and buyer;
- insufficient investments from the participants;
- market failures from private information not shared;
- ineffective bidding mechanisms;
- inappropriate use of confidential information;
- supplier hold-up, expropriation and loss of bargaining power; and
- supplier's private information about its capabilities.

This list above contains many of the salient features but is by no means exhaustive. In order to examine the risks inherent in an organization that is considering outsourcing its IT function, the elements that contribute to the risk in the ITO environment need to be explored. (See also Agency Theory and the Winner's Curse phenomenon in Chapter 4.)

The scope of outsourcing includes strategic IT functions together with value activities that differentiate the organization from its suppliers. As suppliers provide competence in new technologies and access to better IT professionals, these elements contribute strategically to the buyer's organizational value chain. The expanded role of outsourcing relationships includes relatively better services and financial performance, and new lines of business. Elements of the e-commerce value chain, including strategy, systems development and integration, payment processing, market design, advertising and customer management, as well as development of the physical network and web-hosting, are outsourced.

In the ITO scenario, risk carries functions of multiple variables, mathematically expressed as:

Risk = fn(governance, (un)certainty, competitive environment, organizational interconnectedness)

In a 'cause and effect' situation, risks also play a role in the effects of activities engendered by the outsourcing of the IT function. Risks in this instance are concerned with the effect of governance, uncertainty, competitive environment and organizational interconnectedness (Clemons, 2000). The point raised here is that risks in the ITO exercise appear to have a direct relationship with a set of causes. It is argued that, while some arguments for ITO are intuitively appealing at an analytical and general level, they remain simplistic in practice because they do not account for the complexities that permeate the management of information resources and risks (Earl, 1996). Some different models are examined in the following sections.

3.3 IT outsourcing risks (causes and effects)

A primary driver or determinant of risk originates from the lack of information (information asymmetry) in the precontract phase, followed by an inherent inability to accurately monitor the other partner's actions. Further, the conditions of an outsourcing contract allow either the supplier or the buyer to behave opportunistically. Uncertainty, competitive importance and organizational interconnectedness are the other contributory drivers of risk in an ITO exercise. The 'cause' groupings for risks in ITO derive from inabilities to optimally manage the agreement and its subsequent change in line with the evolution and heterogeneity of the IT function.

It has been consistently argued that large, vertically integrated organizations need strategic outsourcing measures to remain competitive, especially in highly contested and fast-moving markets. In a causal chain of events, there are observable causes for risks and, equally, measurable effects should the risks occur. The 'cause' is a situation that exists that sets up a potential risk. The cause of risks can be proactively managed. The effect(s) of risk are the likely outcomes if the risk occurs.

In any outsourcing exercise, risk is an essential and critical component of the formulation of decisions and in the mitigation of its undesirable consequences. In the outsourcing of the IT function, some of the more well documented and major risks involve escalating costs, diminishing service levels, loss of expertise, and contract irreversibility.

Some of the ideas developed in the context of a causal reasoning framework, which is investigated and introduced here, are summarized in Figure 3.4. In this illustration, we assume that the risks in an ITO exercise are caused directly by a set of risk drivers and have a set of effects that are experienced within the organization. In this instance, multiple risk dimensions are possible. The risk types could then lie dormant indefinitely or become manifest in the ITO project. The risk outcomes become the risk exposure for the organization.

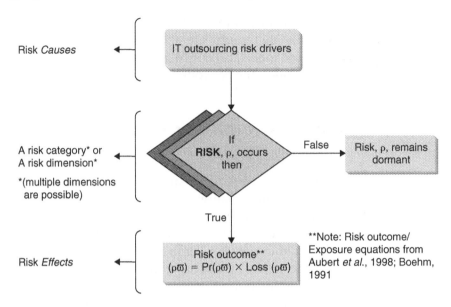

Figure 3.4 Causes and effects of risks in the IT outsourcing exercise (Tho, 2004)

Causality and random activity concept

The causality and random activity concept is of particular importance when determining risks and risk exposure values. Risks should not be dismissed or abandoned on the basis of ambiguity or 'randomness' of risks. One of the most distinctive philosophies of the ancient Greek philosopher and scientist, Aristotle (384–322 BC), was his notion of causality where each action or event has more than one 'reason' that helps to explain what, why, and where things exist. The initial design and thought behind the RDS tool and the research method used was to capture the risks following logical classification into various dimensions.

Following an early view on the subject of causality, the cause of any event is a preceding event or events, without which the event in question would not have occurred. If this rather mechanistic view of causality is translated into context then all the previous actions and events in an ITO exercise would constitute the complete cause of the outcomes of the exercise. It is shown that these effects do not translate into or summarize the risk dimensions that are formulated during the RDS creation exercise. Further investigation in this chapter reveals that the theory of causality breaks down as soon as the inherent complexities in organizations with an intricate set of interdependencies are taken into account. Some of the logic breaks down as soon as random occurrences arise within the framework. Illustrations of the agency theory and simple game theory, discussed in Chapter 4 on the understanding of risk measurements, provide some clues to this end.

The philosophy of causality supports determinism; that is every event has a cause, and the event follows invariably from the cause. This thinking, however, denies the element of chance or contingency. It also does not take into account free will in humanity and the interplay between the sometimes illogical actions of human beings. It is opposed to indifferentism, or indeterminism, which maintains that preceding events do not and cannot definitely determine subsequent ones. Because determinism is generally assumed to be true of all events except volition, the doctrine is of greatest importance when applied to ethics.

Philosophers deny the ultimate reality, or at least the fundamental validity, of the causal relation. Henri Bergson (1927)[1] for example, maintained that neither ultimate reality nor life is bound by exact causal sequences. He propounds that a process of growth takes place in which the unpredictable, and therefore the uncaused, constantly occurs. No exact repetition happens in real time; and where there is no repetition, there is no cause, for cause means that the antecedent is repeatedly followed by the same consequence.

The risk dimensions and RDS formulated identify classic reasons for more work to be done on the relationships between risks dimensions arising in the outsourcing of the IT function as well as major management decisions in today's business environment.

Before the RDS can be used effectively, the direct influences of the operating environment need to be understood. Both exogenous and endogenous risks are accounted for with the method proposed. The participants in and stakeholders of the ITO exercise have information on risks as a perceived set of losses and probabilities. This information is collected and then illustrated using the RDS.

3.4 Measuring risk exposure

Risk exposure has been defined as the extent and probability of an undesirable outcome. If the probability is small, i.e. nearly zero, the risks can be described as almost dormant as they seldom become manifest in the ITO exercise (see the right hand side of Figure 3.4). If a risk type occurs regularly (the box in the lower half of the figure), then it is often recognized as a 'common' risk

---

[1] Nobel Laureate, Nobel prize in Literature, 1927. Found on-line on http://www.nobel.se/literature/laureates/1927/

type. Common risk types have been documented as categories of risks or risk dimensions.

Quantifying risk exposure

There is a common understanding on total risk exposure at a given point in time: it is the mathematical sum of all the risk exposure values. If, however, the risks are classified into different categories, then the sum of the risks occurring in all the categories represents the total risk exposure at a given point in time for the ITO exercise.

The risk exposure is described as the product of the probability and the magnitude of the undesirable outcome from the relationship, as expressed in the equation below.

$$RE = Pr(UO) \times L(UO)$$

where RE is the risk exposure; Pr(UO) is the probability of an undesirable outcome; and L(UO) is the magnitude of loss due to the undesirable outcome.

Considering the variables in the equation above, if the probability (of loss) values were held constant then the risk exposure would be proportional to loss, and vice versa. Practically, however, neither variable (the magnitude of loss nor the probability of loss) is constant over a period of time. So, the total risk exposure for the ITO exercise over time is dynamic (i.e. it changes over time). At any point in time, however, it is the sum of all the risk exposure (RE) values for all the risk elements experienced in the project. Over time, the total risk exposure is represented by the following equation.

Total risk exposure = Total (Probability of loss × Magnitude of loss)

$$\sum_{x=0}^{x \to \infty} Risk\ Exposure = \sum_{x=0}^{x \to \infty} Pr(UO) \cdot L(UO) \qquad (3.1)$$

where $Pr(UO) \cdot L(UO)$ are the individual risk exposure elements.

Risk exposure (RE) boundaries

The probability values provide the parameters that establish the extremities of the equation. The smallest and largest values of probability are zero probability (no chance of occurring) and full probability (definitely occurring). Since the maximum possible value for Pr(UO) is a certainty that the undesirable outcome (UO) will occur, then Pr(UO) = 1. This implies that the maximum, theoretically possible, value of loss due to the undesirable outcome is always less than or equal to the mathematical sum of all possible magnitudes of all the risk elements.

$$\sum_{x=0}^{x \to \infty} Risk\ Exposure_{max} = \sum_{x=0}^{x \to \infty} Pr(UO) \cdot L(UO)_{max} \qquad (3.2)$$

To simplify the equation to a single variable for discussion, both the maximum and minimum values for the probability of loss are taken:

$$\sum_{x=0}^{x \to \infty} Risk\ Exposure_{max} = \sum_{x=0}^{x \to \infty} 1 \cdot L(UO)_{max} \quad \text{Maximum Value}$$

$$\sum_{x=0}^{x \to \infty} Risk\ Exposure_{min} = 0 \qquad\qquad\qquad \text{Minimum Value}$$

$$(3.3)$$

Therefore, given the range of values of probabilities from zero through to a unit (1) it can be reasoned that the total risk exposure is equal to or less than the sum of the total magnitude of loss as a result of undesirable outcomes, illustrated by the next equation below. The maximum value is, theoretically, infinite.

At one selected point in time,

$$\sum_{x=0}^{x \to \infty} Risk\ Exposure \le \sum_{x=0}^{x \to \infty} L(UO) \qquad (3.4)$$

This equation is significant as it describes the relationship between the total risk exposures in an ITO exercise relating to the maximum possible risk exposure values. There is an element of time, in combination with multiple values of loss as a result of risk. An infinite value of total risk exposure is mathematically possible but, practically, is also improbable. By implication, therefore, there must also be a finite number of influences and risk elements that are experienced in an ITO exercise at any single point in time. An infinite number, although theoretically possible, implies again an infinite risk exposure value – a subject for another book. The risk exposure would otherwise have no theoretical limit, i.e. infinite value represented by:

$$\sum_{x=0}^{x \to \infty} L(UO) \qquad\qquad (3.5)$$

In the next section, the possible values for the risk elements are discussed, these values being based on the assumption just made.

3.5 Examples of risk management models

There are numerous risk assessment and risk management models. Two extensively used examples are illustrated here to show commonality in some of the components in the latter. The first example is the model used by the US Government Accounting Office for the management of IT risk (US GAO, 1999). A sample risk management programme is illustrated in Figure 3.5. This model involves an iterative loop that starts with risk assessment (the upper box in Figure 3.5).

Figure 3.5
Sample risk management model A (Source: adapted from the US Government Accounting Office (GAO) document GAO/AIMD-00-33 Information Security Risk Assessment, 1999.)

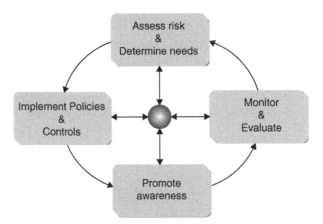

Risk assessment involves identifying possible risks and determining the needs of the particular situation wherein the risk management methods are used. The process then continues with implementation of policies and controls, followed closely by the promotion of awareness of the same risks within the working group or organization. Both awareness and policy actions will be targeted towards mitigating the effects of the risks, should they occur. In an ITO exercise, the same risk assessment and management model is applied. The model assumes that the risks experienced in the exercise are mitigated through a series of actions.

Risk management elements in this model include establishing a central management focal point, implementing appropriate policies and related controls, promoting awareness, and monitoring and evaluating policy and control effectiveness. After risks in an ITO exercise are identified, the appropriate monitoring and evaluation activities work in conjunction with the appropriate governance structures to manage risks. In a mature governance model, policies and controls can be implemented in order to streamline the tasks of risk mitigation.

The second model is used by the organization KPMG[2], and is published as its 'risk maturity framework'. The activities and components are very similar to those of the previously mentioned US Government Accounting Office model. Both models contain elements of determination of risks, followed by measurement and monitoring, then a process for implementing controls and policies. The risk plan or strategy incorporates the overall organizational strategy, which encompasses all the steps outlined above.

Figure 3.6
Sample risk management model B (Source: Adapted and simplified from KPMG Risk Management methodology [Donner, 2001])

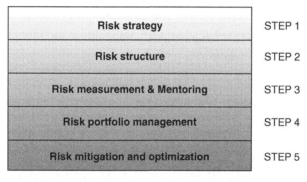

Risk strategy	STEP 1
Risk structure	STEP 2
Risk measurement & Mentoring	STEP 3
Risk portfolio management	STEP 4
Risk mitigation and optimization	STEP 5

The model described in the framework proposed by KPMG appears to take on three active approaches. This includes the reactive, tactical and strategic stance that an organization can adopt as its risk management approach.

Each of these positions will have a plan or approach to risk management that includes the following:

- A risk strategy for associating and managing risks based on the organization's business strategies.
- A risk structure that supports the risk strategy and provides for accountabilities in the structure.

---

[2] KPMG is an international professional services organization that provides risk advisory services

- Measurement and monitoring that establishes measurement criteria and continuous improvement.
- Portfolio management for identifying, assessing and categorizing risks across the organization.
- Optimization to balance potential risks against opportunities within the established portfolio based on the organization's tolerance for risks.

The two models describe a very similar methodology and approach to managing risk. The relationships between the various actions and risk-mitigating activity are monitored as a whole; the risk-reducing effects of one set of risks can often be observed to affect another set of risks. A key point that is raised is the measurement and monitoring of risks using specific criteria from a central component of the risk management models.

The model by KPMG extends the 'actions' component by proposing three types of reaction to risk including reactive, tactical and strategic action plans. These plans, however, are all also dependent on the measurement of risks and risk exposure. The issues arising in the measurement of risks are illustrated in the following section.

3.6 Difficulties in measuring risks and risk exposure

Reliably assessing outsourcing risks can be more difficult than assessing other types of risks. The elements that contribute to the causes of risks are extremely variable in this environment. Project requirements (IT), environment (people) and technology change more quickly in this environment that in any other given the intensity of development in this area (see The role of IT in the organization, Chapter 2). This results in significant shifting in risk profiles for both the supplier and buyer. The lack of reliable and current data makes the determination of outsourcing-risks estimates inconsistent. Risk controls and their extent are often also questionable for the same reason. Because of these limitations, it is important that organizations identify and employ methods that efficiently achieve the benefits of risk assessment while avoiding costly attempts to develop seemingly precise results that are of questionable reliability.

Risks in ITO are often neglected because the effects are not felt by the IT department or the designated area responsible for the operation of ITO. For example, financial risks are sometimes just ignored because the Accounting and Finance department is responsible. Environmental risks that include the effects of competitors, suppliers, and, simply, the operating environment, are also often not considered, simply because they are not included in the purview of the manager's responsibility.

Risk factors are also constantly changing. In an ITO environment where technological change is very rapid and market volatility is high, efficient capacity planning and utilization of internal or fixed assets, for example, need a significant amount of organizational effort. When considering outsourcing elements of the organization, it is this very nature of the effects of risk that must be analysed to be understood and subsequently managed. Delimiting all the ways the possible risks can occur is seldom easy, just as determining the probability of loss is not straightforward. The difficulties are often attributable to problems in obtaining accurate data on probabilities and costs associated with outsourcing risk factors.

The probability of occurrence of an undesirable outcome can be estimated on the basis of past performance characteristics of the risk element, or subjective probabilities already assessed. However, in several areas, probabilities are impossible to assess on the basis of past performance. Consequently, risk assessment methods adopt the approach of approximating the probability of undesirable outcomes by identifying and assessing factors that influence their occurrence. In a software development context, for instance, factors belong to five broad categories: technological newness, application size, lack of expertise on the part of the software development team, application complexity, and organizational environment. The degree to which each factor is present in a software project will contribute to an increase in the probability of the occurrence of an undesirable outcome.

3.7 Measuring IT outsourcing (ITO) risks by group/category

There are various models and methods available for assessing and managing risks, as discussed previously. The scope of the analysis and the amount of resource to be expended varies depending on the type and extent of the assessment to be made. The availability and reliability of data on risk factors and their effects also contribute to determining the type of risk analysis method to be used.

The basic concepts generally involve estimates of the monetary cost of the effects of risk and risk reduction techniques based on:

- the likelihood that a damaging event will occur (probability);
- the costs of potential losses (loss quantum); and
- the costs of mitigating actions that could be taken.

Reliable data on likelihood and costs are often not available and there needs to be a 'feel' of the risks involved as well as the extent of risk exposure that must be borne by the organization in the outsourcing exercise. A qualitative approach can be taken by defining risk in more subjective and general terms such as high, medium and low risk. In this regard, qualitative assessments depend more on the expertise, experience and judgement of those conducting the assessment. It is also possible to use a combination of quantitative and qualitative methods.

The grouping of risks into categories[3] or dimensions is not a new concept. Risk grouping or the classification of risks in a similar category is routinely applied and an integral part of the insurance industry for the purposes of quantifying risks and subsequently defining the insurance premiums to be charged. Actuaries use risk classification to price and design financial security systems. The concept of representing and illustrating the effects of risk in an exercise to outsource the IT function is a derivation of this idea. Risk grouping has the intention of placing individual risks bearing reasonably similar expectations of loss in a group or class of risks. This exercise estimates risks from probabilities associated with the occurrence, timing and magnitude of events using concepts borrowed from the insurance industry in its classification of risk profiles.

The term causality referred to above is not used in the strictest or rigorous sense of cause and effect, but in a general sense, i.e. where there is a plausible relationship between the characteristics of a risk grouping and the hazard for which an outsourcing activity or task is provided. For example, outsourcing the maintenance of the customer database would not by itself cause loss of privacy or data, but it does bear a reasonable relationship to the risk hazard of operational risk, and thus would be a reasonable basis for grouping risks for the outsourcing of the IT function. The concept is nevertheless important when considering

---

[3] American Actuarial Standard of Practice (ASOP) No. 12, (1990), *Concerning Risk Classification*, Actuarial Standards Board (ASB), 15th January, 1990

the individual elements of risk categories (see also the Case Study example in Chapter 8).

Considering types of risk will help in classifying them into groups (i.e. categories or dimensions) as a method of quantifying, reducing or simplifying the many risks in any particular outsourcing arrangement. This is not to say that risks are going to be 'boxed' or can be encapsulated into categories, as this would be grossly misleading. The intention, however, is to be able to simplify the understanding of all of the risks that occur during the different phases of an ITO exercise in order to be able to manage, manipulate and reduce the effects of risks. By classifying risks in specific groupings, the risk landscape will be more easily understood.

3.8 So why group risks?

It is both impossible and unnecessary to predict what the experience would be for individual risks in all activities concerned in the outsourcing of the IT function. There are a finite number of risk elements that contribute to the total risk exposure in an ITO exercise. In addition, if the occurrence, timing and magnitude of an event were known in advance, there would be no economic uncertainty and therefore no reason for management of uncertainty. Predictions of risk experience in 'groups or classes of risk' provide a sufficient compromise, as data on experiencing individual risk elements are not deemed to be accurate.

Associating similar risk types

Estimates are typically made through the use of past experience, coupled with projections of future trends, for groups with similar risk characteristics. The grouping of risks with similar risk characteristics builds and maintains an equitable system regarding the pricing system that determines insurance premiums. This concept of grouping of risks to determine averages and the application of these averages is also used to classify risks in the determination of risks for the outsourcing of the IT function.

A difficulty in risk classification derives from trying to handle issues of 'fairness' and 'similar risk characteristics'. The assumption, based on experience, is that every outsourcing activity, individual, business (even within one industry group), and outsourcing contract is unique. This makes any particular risk classification process unworkable to the extent that the risk classification process attempts to identify and measure every characteristic of every activity engaged in by the organization. On the other hand, as there are differences in risk characteristics between contracts and between businesses that bear significantly upon cost, to ignore all such differences would be 'unfair'. These issues compound the difficulty surrounding risk classification as it is not clear where lines should be drawn.

Evaluating over time

Defining the uncertainty of an occurrence and of its timing, and of the magnitude of a particular event, albeit in this process with a price peg, does not make the unquantified known; nor need it. By outsourcing the IT function, the organization assumes the financial uncertainty. It is not able to 'fix' the occurrence or the magnitude of a specific risk merely because it assumes that risk. With a price tag on risk, it would be easier to make decisions during the process of evaluating options in the outsourcing exercise. One way to estimate a price is to rely exclusively on heuristics, i.e. experience, insight and judgement concerning the nature of the particular hazard involved and the exposure to loss. This method is not optimal but reveals the 'recentness' of the concepts in complete outsourcing of the IT function (historical data are scarce, and often do not even exist). A more critical approach would be, theoretically, to observe the actual losses associated with the risk over an extended period of time. The nature of the risks identified here is unique. Hindsight often suggests there is little or no cost as the individual risk within the IT environment moves to a likely or even certain eventual realization. Hazards change so rapidly over the period of observation that the information obtained by past observations may not be applicable to the current or future exposure to financial uncertainty. The development of IT and the changing nature of this industry are a subject of a separate discussion.

Considering risk characteristics and focus

An alternative method of grouping risk would be to observe the losses associated with groups of individual risks with similar characteristics, which frequently can be done over a more acceptable period of time. The notion of risk groups is identified with this concept. While any individual risk in a given class is no more predictable than it was before the transferring or pooling of the risk occurred, a reasonable price may be established by observing the losses of the group of risks and relating the price to the average experience of the group. Perfect conditions are seldom achieved. The risk characteristics defined here hence reflect both observed fact and informed judgement. The method used to collect data on the probability and magnitude of loss is described in the next chapter.

Risk classification

Risks encountered in the outsourcing of the IT function and their effects on the organization such as higher cost levels, degraded service levels and loss of expert resources have been identified from past experience and discussed in various formats as well as in the literature. It is recognized that the probability of occurrence and loss resulting from the undesirable outcome can be effectively mitigated by early identification of the risk areas and formulating specific strategies. Risk mitigation therefore actively seeks to reduce undesirable consequences by implementing risk-reducing measures and disaster-recovery plans already in place for rapid deployment.

Insurance, for example, is commonly used to mitigate the economic uncertainty associated with chance occurrences. 'Insurance exchanges the uncertainty of the occurrence, the timing, and the financial impact of a particular event for a predetermined price.' (Actuarial Standards Board, 1989; American Academy of Actuaries, 1980, p. 2.)

Risk classification is used to group individual risks having reasonably similar expectations of loss. It is important to note that the determination of an average experience for a particular class of risk is not the same as predicting the experience for an individual risk in the class. It is not humanly possible and is, arguably, unnecessary, to predict experience for individual risks. In this exercise, the risk groups or classes occurring in the outsourcing of the IT function are brought together. Observation of interaction between the risk groups are then used to derive strategies for maintaining an 'equal' risk profile based on acceptable levels of risk or acceptable tolerance levels for the particular exercise.

The classifications of risks are used to illustrate, for example, the risk groupings and negotiation strategies between the buyer and supplier. Information on the interaction of risk groups becomes input for the initial decision to select a suitable outsource supplier. It is also important that this information is available for decisions on ongoing governance of the ITO arrangement. A point of equilibrium in the risk profiles is sought. In this exercise, the organization's tolerance for risk and compromises can then be supported by a set of tangible risk profiles, which are discussed in this chapter.

3.9 Identifying risk groups for IT outsourcing (ITO)

If risks are to be grouped, the next task is to identify the risk groups that should be used. Although the risks identified in the previous section specifically address some risk areas, larger risks groupings have been identified through the use of subject headers such as financial, business, technical, strategic, operations, and political areas of risks (DiRomualdo and Gurbaxani, 1998). The risk groups observed earlier can be classified under financial risk and operational risk types. Business, strategic, and political risks have involved new business start-ups, process re-engineering, refocus on the client's core competencies, assistance in managing mergers or globalization, and diminishing the often political debates about new IT projects (Sobol and Apte, 1998). The technical risks commonly offered have included access to expertise, improved services, new technologies, and technological innovation (Kern and Willcocks, 2001). The risks often accompany benefits in similar situations and similar areas.

For use in an ITO project for example, list of risk categories will be determined. This list is specific to and characteristic of the ITO project. Risk profiles of all ITO projects differ. The approach normally used is to group risks by proposing frameworks that segment the types of ITO related risk for analysis (Clemons, 1995; Earl, 1996).

Recommended risk groups/dimensions

A common set of eleven risk elements or areas that are most exposed or prone to undesirable outcomes were used. These areas appear in the majority of ITO projects; they are listed on the left of the table in Table 3.1. For the purposes of describing the risk groups accurately, the term **risk dimensions** is used.

Along with these risk elements, the risk groups[4] are arranged in a matrix. The technical risk group for example, covers elements

---

[4] Which can also be called risk categories or risk dimensions with synonymous meaning

Table 3.1 Example of mapping risk elements into categories or dimensions (Tho, 2004)

Risk elements (Source: Earl, 1996)	Risk categories/Dimensions							
	Technical	Financial	Legal	Operational	Business	Environmental	Information	Strategic
Possibility of weak management				✓				
Inexperienced staff								
Business uncertainty		✓			✓		✓	
Outdated technology skills	✓					✓	✓	✓
Endemic uncertainty		✓	✓				✓	✓
Hidden costs		✓	✓				✓	
Lack of organizational learning				✓			✓	
Loss of innovative capacity	✓						✓	
Dangers of eternal triangle			✓			✓		
Technological indivisibility	✓		✓	✓		✓		✓
Fuzzy focus			✓			✓		✓

Risk elements (Source: Earl, 1996)

like outdated technology skills, loss of innovative capacity and technological indivisibility. As each risk group is mapped against the elements shown in Table 3.1, the accuracy of the risk groups is verified. For each risk group proposed, each of the risk elements is cross-checked against the others. This approach assists in quickly identifying possible risk groups or dimensions. There is only one checkpoint for the business risks category. The data here suggest that this category would capture the 'other' risk factors that would arise in the data collection of risk elements.

The same risk elements, once identified, enable actions to be taken that mitigate risks. This adds a focus to the possibilities of failure on the decision on whether to outsource or not. The risks of not outsourcing, interestingly, carry similar risk factors. The focus is on the risks of outsourcing of the IT function. These risk areas can also be mapped into the categories or dimensions proposed in Table 3.1.

Risk categories and risk types vary between projects. In another project for example, ten groupings of risk identified were financial, technical, project, political, contingency, non-use, internal abuse, external abuse, competitive, reputation, and governmental. These risk groups are, again, collections of risk elements of similar nature. In this example ideas of possible trade-offs between the risk areas or groups was raised. This is an important assumption that is carried forward in the development of the interrelationships between such risk groups. These groups can be mapped into the eight that have been proposed in Table 3.1.

In considering the risk dimensions, the ability to predict and anticipate an undesirable event occurring is important since the consequences of this event are irreversible. Proactive action can be taken by focusing on the data that are used to determine the events or activities that influence these probabilities. For example, by choosing a reputable supplier, the outsourcing project has a lower probability of failure.

Technological newness, application size, lack of expertise on the part of the software development team, application complexity, and organizational environment have been contributory events to the possible failure of software development. The extent of influence of each event in a software project will contribute to the increased probability of the occurrence of an undesirable outcome (that is, project failure).

3.10 Visualizing risk patterns from arbitrary risk dimensions

The task of presenting the risk data in a meaningful and easily understandable format needs to be addressed to assess the risk profile. To do this, the information on the probability and risk exposure form data points that are plotted along multiple risk dimensions.

Linking risk dimensions with operational and relationship risks

A summary of the risk dimensions based on previous work in the area of unwanted outcomes is then distilled down to costs and changes in scope, which leads to the following eight risk groups along three risk dimensions (i.e. financial, operational and legal) proposed in Table 3.2.

Table 3.2 Proposed risk groupings for IT outsourcing based on evidence of loss as a result of risk elements described in this section

Dimension	Description	Characteristic	Influence
C1	Technical	*Possible loss from the use of existing and new technology* – Complexity of the new and emerging technology and interfaces – Uncertainty – Technological discontinuity – Task complexity	Internal
C2	Financial	*Possible loss from unbudgeted events* – Lack of experience and expertise of the enterprise with the activity – Lack of planning and inaccurate budgeting – Uncertainty	Internal
C3	Legal	*Possible loss from legal disagreements or legal challenges* – Lack of experience and expertise of the enterprise with the activity – Lack of experience of the client with outsourcing – Uncertainty about the legal environment	External/ internal
C4	Operational	*Possible loss from poor operations quality or mishap* – Lack of experience and expertise of the client with contract management – Measurement problems – Lack of experience and expertise of the supplier with the activity	Internal

continued

Table 3.2   continued

Dimension	Description	Characteristic	Influence
C5	**Business**	*Possible loss from adverse changes in business* – Asset specificity – Small number of suppliers – Scope – Interdependence of activities	External
C6	**Environment**	*Possible loss from factors external to organization* – Measurement problems – Lack of experience and expertise of the organization and/or of the supplier with OS contracts – Poor cultural fit	External
C7	**Information**	*Possible loss from insufficient or inaccurate information* – Interdependence of activities – Lack of experience and expertise of the supplier with the activity – Supplier size – Supplier financial stability – Measurement problems – Task complexity	External
C8	**Strategic**	*Possible loss from errors in direction or tactical mistakes* – Loss of organizational competency – Scope – Proximity of the core competencies – Interdependence of activities	Internal/ external

Financial risks
1. Management costs (unbudgeted/unbudgetable transition costs)
2. Lock-in (switching costs)
3. Hidden costs (uncertainty and absence of complete information)
4. Increased cost of services.

Operational/Legal risks
5. Contract amendments
6. Disputes and litigation
7. Loss of competency(ies)
8. Service debasement.

Illustrating risk exposure

In this example, taking the eight risk groups proposed and illustrated in Table 3.2, and values for the probability of an undesirable outcome as well as loss due to the undesirable outcome, we derive the sample data illustrated in Table 3.3.

Table 3.3 Sample data for measurement of risk exposure

	Transition/Management costs	Lock-in	Contractual amendments	Disputes & Litigation	Service debasement	Increased cost of services	Loss of organizational competencies	Hidden costs
Risk exposure	14	18	29.25	27.5	21	19.2	28.8	24.5
Probability of undesirable outcome	2.8	4.5	6.5	5.5	3.5	4	6	7
Loss due to undesirable outcome	5	4	4.5	5	6	4.8	4.8	3.5

Adapted from Aubert *et al.*, 1998, with arbitrary values for Probability and Loss Magnitude in this example

Each risk group carries information on risk exposure. The risk exposure comprises elements of the probability of undesirable outcomes (on a probability scale) and the magnitude of losses (on a financial scale) owing to undesirable outcomes. Using the relationship equation defined earlier (i.e. the product of the probability and loss magnitude) the risk exposure values in each of the risk groups can be plotted (see Figure 3.7).

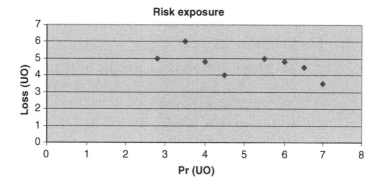

Figure 3.7
Risk exposure as a function of the Pr (UO) and Loss (UO). (With values from Table 3.3.)

The graph in Figure 3.7 illustrates the risk exposure as defined by the example scenario described. In this example, if the loss due to the undesirable outcomes were held constant but probabilities (other than the maximum and minimum value) were reduced to 1 (or 10%), then the effects of the shape of the curve as a result of reduced risk exposure would be that shown in Figure 3.8.

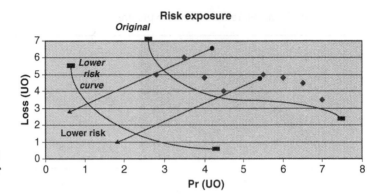

Figure 3.8
As risk exposure reduces, the graph indicates changes (in the direction of the arrows) inwards the lower left corner of the chart

As risk exposure values change, different methods are used to manage the risks that occur. These methods make use of the information (see Figure 3.7 and Figure 3.8) from this framework to measure and illustrate the changes before and after management actions have been taken.

The common method used for representing multivariable data via two-dimensional charts illustrates key movements of risk exposure along the key dimensions. A possible limitation here is the ability to illustrate risk movements along the key groupings of risk. The accuracy of the data that describe the risk exposure as a result of the difficulties in measuring probability and loss magnitude also affects the results. By collecting the risk elements into groups or risk dimensions, the qualitative examination of the risks include, rather arbitrarily, the collective risks along any one grouping. This is not to say that the accuracy of the results has improved. By grouping the risks, the errors are also grouped.

The shape of the 'curve' formed by the graph is described as the risk profile. The term risk profile describes the unique shape or contour that is formed when the risk exposure data points are plotted. A new risk profile for the risks in the outsourcing exercise is observed when the risks are plotted against the eight risk dimensions in Table 3.2. The tool described then can be used to illustrate a risk profile at one point in time. This allows separate risk profiles to be compared.

Mapping possible risk dimensions against the risk landscape

To establish the relevant risk dimensions for analysis, other perspectives of risk are reviewed. An alternative perspective of risk is to equate it to the variance of the distribution of outcomes. The extent of the variability in results (whether positive or negative) is the measure of risk. Risk is sometimes also defined as the volatility of a portfolio of activities and its value. This technique is borrowed from the area of finance where 'the highest expected return for a given level of risk, and the lowest level of risk for a given expected return' applies (Schirripa and Tecotsky, 2000). Here, risk exposure is also defined as both a loss and a probability function.

Another variant in the perspective of risks from these definitions and arguments is the popularized and widely used balanced scorecard proposed by Norton and Kaplan (1996); four risk 'perspectives' are derived: financial, customer, internal and innovation and learning risks. Similarly, additional risk sets or types of risks that affect inter-organizational information systems (IOIS) include technical, asset, organizational, and environmental risk. There are project, capability, financial, and maintainability risks, caused by a variety of technical, organizational, and environmental factors (Sherer, 1995). These risk sets then extend to more subtle risk sets.

For the purposes of this exercise, a hybrid meaning in the grouping of risks is used. The concepts described here are adapted with input from the various other perspectives discussed. As the risks and risk exposure information will be collected and measured, the term 'risk dimension' more accurately depicts the new meaning and intention. A risk dimension will show a grouping of risks with similar business function and expectation of loss. The following provides descriptions of the risk dimensions that will be used (see also Table 3.2).

Technical risk (C1 in Table 3.2) is a combination of risks resulting from the use of technology. Besides the characteristics listed in Table 3.2, other possible losses in this area could derive from interconnectivity problems and as more open systems are developed, key technical risks arise from security issues.

A major category of risks is in the Financial dimension (C2 in Table 3.2). The losses occurring as a result of poor planning and experience are major contributors to losses in this group when outsourcing the IT function. To guard against variation clauses in outsourcing contracts, specialized techniques are employed including the use of instruments like additional resource charges (ARCs) and reduced resource charges (RRCs) to accommodate fluctuations in demand from that specified in the capacity plan. This leads to the next risk dimension.

The use of agreements and legal instruments is designed to mitigate risks along most of the risk groups. Legal risks (C3 in Table 3.2) themselves, however, are significant as a result of increasing use of agreements and contracts.

Operational risk (C4 in Table 3.2) includes possible losses in operations when the supplier takes over responsibility for the outcomes. It is typical for the risks in this dimension to be 'passed on' from the buyer to the supplier organization when the outsourcing contract is activated. The shifting risk has been described earlier.

Outsourcing involves a close partnership between two or more organizations. Business risks (C5 in Table 3.2) arise from the relationship between the partners operating in an environment where there is also interaction between other competing organizations, threat of substitute products, competitive barriers to entry and exit, and competitor rivalry. Environmental risks (C6 in Table 3.2) are closely related to the business risks and become manifest as a result of factors external to the organization. Environmental risk includes dependence risk, where one organization becomes dependent on another that attempts to change the terms of the contract or fails to perform adequately, and competitive risk, where one organization attempts to 'steal' competitive information from another. With more-open systems in rapidly changing environments and the use of information technology's monitoring capabilities, dependence risk will decrease. However, competitive risk will become more significant as functionality and accessibility of shared information increases.

Informational risk (C7 in Table 3.2) is very significant when the IT function is outsourced. The worst-case scenario would be a complete loss of the organization's information. Other losses are incurred as a result of inaccurate or insufficient information when a third party manages the IT function.

Finally, the strategic risks (C8 in Table 3.2) involve tactical mistakes made by the organization in outsourcing the IT function itself. An example of a significant tactical mistake would be when a supplier organization begins to 'leak' sensitive information relating to the organization to the latter's competitors. The outsourcing of the data component and the selection of the supplier are the tactical decisions made that resulted in the loss.

Risks are associated with all forms of outsourcing decisions. The risk 'signature' for the buyer of outsourcing services is larger than that for the supplier in the majority of cases. The risk profile reflects the importance of the relationship and the sharing of the risk profiles. While significant client/external service provider (ESP) interdependency is not in itself a risk, the risks to the client organization may increase when disagreements emerge about the provision of outsourcing services. To the extent that some large-scale IT sourcing deals are successful, others are less so. Service level agreements (SLAs) and other forms of service contracts specify a series of measurable activities that suppliers provide.

Outsourcing can generate new risks, such as the loss of critical skills or developing the wrong skills, the loss of cross-functional skills, and the loss of control over suppliers. Also, outsourcing has led to a loss of skills and corporate memory. These risks are especially pertinent when the supplier's priorities do not match the buyer's requirements. Short-term contracts, based on the principle of the lowest winning bid, stifle incentives to innovate because rewards for innovation cannot be secured by the supplier.

3.11 Constructing the signature

The eight risk dimensions shown in Table 3.2 are proposed as the starting point, for the majority of ITO projects, to analyse the basic risk sets that will be used to construct the risk profile. Each time these dimensions are used, they should be reviewed and analysed for relevance and accuracy. This exercise should always be done, especially if the organization in question is from another industry or the scope of the IT function being outsourced is different. The risk profile would illustrate all the risk dimensions (comprising the total risk exposure for the outsourcing exercise) on one diagram.

3.12 Graph types

To do this, several options and visualization techniques were reviewed including the star graph, radar plot and stereo-ray glyphs of Carr and Nicholson (1998). The star plot, for example, was tested as a means of showing multivariate visualization or risk dimensions in which the multiple measurements of risk exposure would be plotted on equally spaced radii extending from the centre of a circle and linked to form a star. In the radar plot, these radii also represented the value of the measurement. In this instance, however, each radius stands for a risk dimension instead of a variable. The risk (dimension) response, the risk exposure on each variable, is displayed by points of different shapes or colours, or both.

The risk exposure values in Table 3.3 and Figure 3.7 are re-plotted using the radar graph in Figure 3.9. The risk profile now describes the risk exposure along multiple axes representing risk dimensions. The resulting risk profile illustration is unique for an ITO project at any given point in time. For reference, this profile will be called the '**risk signature**' (see Figure 3.9).

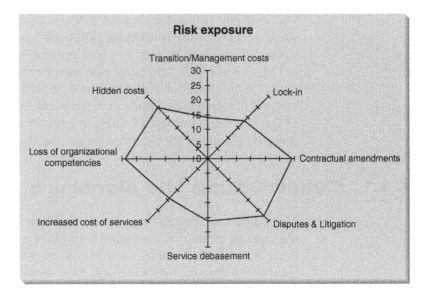

Figure 3.9
The risk signature or radar plot of risk exposure with reference to Table 3.3 and Figure 3.7

The risk signature illustrates the sum of all the risk exposure values derived from the tools previously proposed. What was not obvious through the linear diagrams (Table 3.3 and Figure 3.7) is more easily observed with the multivariate graph. The area bounded by the curve in Figure 3.8 will therefore also represent the total risk exposure experienced by the organization at that point in time.

An assessment of the overall risk exposure along each of the eight risk dimensions would allow the changes in risk exposure along one dimension (a group of risks with similar characteristics) to be manifested on another dimension. This will prompt answers to questions such as, 'What are the effects of reducing the risk of transition costs[5], for example on the risks in organizational competencies through more attention to the skills being outsourced?' or 'What are the effects of reducing the risk

---

[5] Where transition costs are the costs that are incurred at the time the supplier takes over the IT outsourcing function

exposure to disputes and litigation if we paid more attention to the services (increasing the relatively low risk on costs of services)?'

In the case of a reduction in risk exposure, the area enclosed by the curve would simply decrease proportionately. The risk exposure of transition cost escalation for example is not nearly as high as that for contract amendments of loss of organizational competencies. The graph shows the frequencies of data series relative to one another. The correlation of one dimension to another is also visible, i.e. where there is a relationship between the risk dimensions.

Three methods can be considered for preparing the scales along each of the axes on the graphs as the data on risk exposure are captured. These options are measurement in categorical, in rank-ordered and in continuous format.

Categorical scales on the axes

When the categorical scales (or nominal scales) are used to quantify the risks, the values in each dimension are taken by tallying up the numbers along each of the risk dimensions. For example, the values are made up of two components, i.e. high- and low-risk items. Other variables with more than two categories including medium–high, very high, medium–low and very low, are also plotted on the categorical scales. This method provides an illustration of the risk profiles. It may be too inaccurate to indicate changes in the risk profile/signature as a result of changes made in the outsourcing exercise. To be of any use, the risk profile requires more-accurate readings to allow a meaningful analysis of changes in risk and for a comparison of different profiles.

Rank-ordered scales on the axes

The second method uses rank-ordered scales (or ordinal scales), which quantify each dimension by giving each data point a rank. For example, the eight dimensions might be ranked from 1 to 8 in terms of order of risk severity. The dimensions would be ranked 1st, 2nd, 3rd, 4th, etc. in a rank-ordered scale. This option would serve to provide relative risk weightings of the individual dimensions in terms of criticality and need for attention. This would be used to prioritize management attention along the dimensions but is not useful in the examination or comparison of the different profiles. Data on the relative weightings may then be collected from interviews with individual personnel involved with the outsourcing exercise. There is little consensus, however, with regard to the relative weighting of each dimension.

Likert scales on the axes

The third method uses continuous scales, which quantify the qualitative assessment risk severity at equal intervals along a 5-point yardstick. The scale information would be scored against the criteria as follows:

No risk   = 1
Little risk   = 2
Expected risk   = 3
High risk   = 4
Very high risk   = 5
Unacceptable risk = 6

The Likert scale, with a numeric index of 1 to 6 based on an empirical severity of the exposure to risk, was used. A '1' would represent no risk, and a '6' unacceptable risk. Given the subjective nature of the assessment, an even number has been allocated to the Likert scale to avoid 'fence sitting' and force the results of the evaluation to either side of the risk scale. This method of collecting data was the most effective. This is discussed further in the next chapter along with the methods employed to acquire the data for the risk signature diagrams.

3.13 IT outsourcing and the risk dimension signature (RDS)

A 'risk signature', as defined previously, is derived from the pattern of risk exposure along the dimensions of an arbitrary eight risk dimensions that provides an intuitive interface to allow further assessment and analysis. The risk signature, comprising the risk exposure values along each risk dimension, also shows the total risk exposure experienced in the outsourcing exercise.

The characteristics of the risk dimension describe each risk dimension and the rationale for selecting the individual risk elements to be grouped into the risk dimensions. The 'influence' provides clues as to the origin of the causes, as illustrated in Figure 3.2. Following the construction of the RDS, the risk profile needs to be illustrated and salient messages translated or understood. This is the subject of the following chapter.

4 The challenge of understanding risks when outsourcing the IT function

Where observation is concerned, chance favours only the prepared mind.
Louis Pasteur (1822–1895), French scientist
At an Inauguration lecture, Faculty of Science, University of Lille

Digital tools magnify the abilities that make us unique in the world: the ability to think, the ability to articulate our thoughts, the ability to work together to act on those thoughts.
Bill Gates (1955–), US business executive

The risks that occur in an IT outsourcing (ITO) exercise are complex and understanding the interaction of risks after measuring the varieties of risks can be a daunting task. It is important for a manager in this situation, therefore, to be able to visualize (metaphorically) the intensity and range of current risks in order to effectively control activities and determine the outcomes. This involves the ability to understand risk exposure. To do so, it is necessary to be able to appreciate the quantitative nature of risks, compare risks (and changes) over time, observe risk patterns and then actively reduce the effects of selected risk elements. As has already been highlighted in Section I, many risks originate from failures to successfully monitor the relationship between supplier and buyer, the element of uncertainty in the IT function itself, the level of competitive importance that has been imposed on the IT function that is being outsourced, and the level of interconnectedness between the buyer and supplier organizations.

Risks in ITO are unwelcome. Risks represent the worst that could happen, especially when the benefits and reasons why an organization used ITO could be jeopardized or the success of the enterprise could be threatened. There would be a successful outcome when buyers of ITO services have the IT products and services delivered both on time and to budget. Likewise, suppliers want to deliver to the buyer's expectations. Risks, therefore, are an inherent component of ITO and must be understood in order to be mitigated.

In this chapter, the notion of a 'portrait' of the risk landscape for the ITO exercise will be introduced from the RDS illustrations constructed in Chapter 3. The 'risk portrait' is a description of all the risks that are exhibited during an ITO exercise. It is displayed with the use of star graph, radar plot and stereo-ray glyphs. It can be used also as an instrument to illustrate complex risks. In a graphical format, the risk portrait communicates the risk complexity in a manageable format to the person working on risks in this environment. With this, the shifting of risks between supplier and buyer that was discussed previously in Section I can be observed with the oscillation between both buyer and supplier entities.

Also, in order to understand, manage and mitigate the complex and varied risks that become manifest, the concept of 'grouped risks' or 'categorization' is borrowed from the insurance industry in the formulation of its insurance products and premiums. The 'risk portrait' introduced illustrates the changes in the nature and severity of risks, over time, as both the supplier and buyer of ITO services interact. To measure and show risk exposure, the risk categories are collected and assembled into risk portfolios that provide a set of comprehensive information on risks for both the supplier and buyer of ITO services. This notion extends further to enable the illustration and comparison of the various interactions or relationships between actions in a typical ITO scenario. It is shown that the information can then subsequently be used as a means to plan negotiations that aim to arrive at more-equitable ITO arrangements between the buyer and supplier organizations. This tool is called the risk dimension signature or RDS (Tho, 2003) (see below).

4.1 Interpreting the RDS

A risk signature can also be construed to mean a particular risk profile that is created using a number of different methods. To differentiate the risk signature that is constructed from risk dimensions, the term **risk dimension signature** (RDS) is coined. It is an imprint of the risks from risk dimensions or groups already identified for a specific ITO arrangement. The risk dimension signature represents a unique picture of the risks at one point in time during the ITO project. It uniquely differentiates the project from any other. It would be very unlikely for two identical RDS patterns to co-exist.

The risk signature is a tool that will assist the organization to better understand risks to business operations and avoid risky practices, such as allowing scope creep and development of a variety of alternative supplier practices, and to be alert for other events streaming from agency theory. It also provides an efficient means for communicating assessment findings and recommended actions to business unit managers as well as to senior corporate officials. Standard report formats and the periodic nature of the assessments have provided organizations with a means of readily understanding reported information and comparing results among units over time. The RDS will be the primary tool to support the notion that there is a set of interrelationships between the actions and effects of actions that influence the risks.

When the risk profiles for both the supplier and buyer are superimposed on the same chart, the relative risk exposures also reveal areas where negotiations for trading one party's risk for another can be made. In Figure 4.1 for example, the buyer-risks (indicated using the solid line) along risk dimensions A, B, D, E, F and H are relatively larger than those of the supplier (indicated using dotted lines), which are seen as having a relatively 'safe' risk profile. Along dimensions C and G however, the supplier is more at risk relative to the buyer organization.

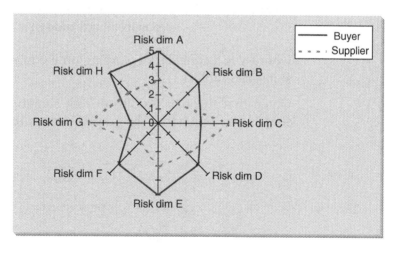

Figure 4.1
Examples of dissimilar signatures (or risk dimension signatures) of the buyer and supplier organizations along eight arbitrary risk dimensions

A more detailed discussion can follow, given more information on the nature of the risk dimensions; the buyer could trade some the risks in A, B, D, E, F and H for C and G.

While it is clear that the buyer experiences more risk along the dimensions along the vertical axes, and the supplier has increased risk along the dimensions on the horizontal axes, a question that needs to be asked is if the total risk exposure for the buyer and the supplier is the same. Knowing that the area bounded by the risk signature reveals the total risk exposure for the buyer and supplier organizations in this example of an outsourcing agreement, the total risk exposure can be measured and computed (see next section).

4.2 Computation of total risk exposure

To compute the area bounded by the risk signature or profile, the formula for the area under the curve, given multiple dimensions (eight in this case), is constructed from basic mathematical principles. The angle between each risk dimension, *A* through *H*, is 45°, derived from 360° divided by eight (corresponding to the number of equal angles). Hence the *total risk*, or area enclosed by the graph under this profile, can easily be computed as in equation (4.1) below.

Total risk = Area enclosed by the graph
(risk here represents the risk exposure, RE)

therefore

Total risk = α [Σ (product of adjacent risk
exposure magnitudes)] (4.1)

where α is a constant depending on the number of risk dimensions (see Table 4.1).

Given that the risk profiles or risk signatures are multi-sided shapes, the area under the graph is computed as follows.

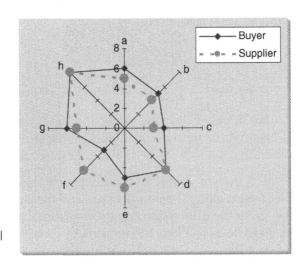

Figure 4.2
Sample risk signature (RDS) demonstrating key values for the computation of total risk exposure

$$\sum \text{risk} = 0.5\sin\theta \left[\sum_{i=1}^{i=7} (\text{risk}_i \times \text{risk}_{(i+1)}) + (\text{risk}_1 \times \text{risk}_8) \right]$$

But $\theta = 45°$ where there are 8 dimensions therefore,

$$\sum \text{risk} = \alpha \left[\sum_{i=1}^{i=7} (\text{risk}_i \times \text{risk}_{(i+1)}) + (\text{risk}_1 \times \text{risk}_8) \right]$$

where $\alpha = 0.3536$

The total risk exposure changes are the total risk profile changes. When the number of risk dimensions change, then the value of the constant α also changes, where

$\alpha = \sin [360/(\# \text{ risk dimensions})]$

Table 4.1 illustrates the possible values of α given the changes in the number of risk dimensions.

Table 4.1 Sample computation of the constant α for use in the computation of the total risk exposure in a construct of the risk profile in equation (4.1) and as illustrated in Figure 4.2

No of risk dimensions	3	4	5	6	7	8	9
Angle theta	120	90	72	60	51	45	40
Constant alpha	0.4330	0.5000	0.4755	0.4330	0.3909	0.3536	0.3214

The number of risk dimensions in Table 4.1 ranges from three to nine. To graphically illustrate risk, or negative outcomes, eight selected dimensions of risk were arbitrarily chosen. These dimensions were plotted along equally spaced axes, all at 45° angles in a radar plot. These dimensions were selected based on a rationale for classifying risks into categories. In proposing eight risk dimensions (see Table 3.2), the number 8 rather coincidentally matched the optimal value. This is supported by Miller (1994): while discussing the bandwidth dilemma in data representation, he introduced the rule of 'seven plus and minus two' during the presentation on multivariate, multidimensional visualization techniques. Keller and Keller (1993) also endorsed this rule during their discussion on radar and spider plots. This appears to be the optimal number of risk dimensions to visualize or depict the risk profile of an outsourcing project. Also, as will be seen in the following sections, it is observed that 8 seems to be the optimal number of risk dimensions representative of a collection of many risks of a similar nature.

As mentioned in Chapter 1, visualization is a process of balancing noise and smoothness. Instead of following some generalized cognitive rules, we should process data representation along the noise–smoothness continuum owing to different research goals and data types.

Comparing buyer and supplier risks on the RDS

From the RDS example in Figure 4.2, the total risk exposure for the buyer's risk exposure is computed as 82.4 and the supplier's risk exposure as 82.05 using the following formulae derived from equation (4.1). The actual computation is shown here.

Buyer risk

$$\Sigma \mathbf{risk} = 0.5 \times 0.7071 \: [(\text{Dim A.Dim B}) + (\text{Dim B.Dim C})$$
$$+ (\text{Dim C.Dim D}) + (\text{Dim D.Dim E})$$
$$+ (\text{Dim E.Dim F}) + (\text{Dim F.Dim G})$$
$$+ (\text{Dim G.Dim H}) + (\text{Dim H.Dim A})]$$
$$= 0.5 \times 0.7071 \: (30 + 20 + 24 + 30 + 15 + 18 + 48 + 48)$$
$$= \mathbf{82.4}$$

Supplier risk

$$\Sigma \mathbf{risk} = 0.5 \times 0.7071 \: [(\text{Dim A.Dim B}) + (\text{Dim B.Dim C})$$
$$+ (\text{Dim C.Dim D}) + (\text{Dim D.Dim E})$$
$$+ (\text{Dim E. Dim F}) + (\text{Dim F.Dim G})$$
$$+ (\text{Dim G.Dim H}) + (\text{Dim H.Dim A})]$$
$$= 0.5 \times 0.7071 \: (20 + 12 + 18 + 36 + 36 + 30 + 40 + 40)$$
$$= \mathbf{82.05}$$

Interpreting the buyer and supplier RDSs

From the RDS in Figure 4.2, it is also quantitatively or empirically observed that both the supplier and buyer experience almost identical[1] total risk exposure from the outsourcing arrangement. When the charts are analysed from the perspective of the risk dimensions however, the supplier is over-exposed along risk dimensions E and F. The buyer, on the other hand, carries more risk along all the remaining risk dimensions. The supplier hence

---

[1] The difference between 82.4 and 82.05 is insignificant for this purpose

carries an advantage along all but two of the risk dimensions. This would otherwise be unknown if it was not charted. The increase in risk is not linear but a quadratic function indicating increasing exposure on the part of the organization.

If the magnitude of risk exposure (RE_ξ) along any one dimension changes, the difference in total risk profile to the organization or organization project is:

$$(R.E._\xi - \delta R.E._\xi) \times \Sigma \text{ (product of adjacent R.E. magnitudes)} \times \lambda$$
$$(4.2)$$

where λ is a constant given the risk profile, and ξ defines the risk categories.

Equation (4.2) is the same as equation (4.1) except that it shows the difference and change in the total risk exposure. This means also that when risk dimensions are held constant, i.e. Σ (adjacent RE) $\times \lambda$, the risk profile relationship is linear or can also be measured directly from either the probability or magnitude of risk exposure, i.e. read directly from the axes of risk dimensions. This is worth while noting for making simple analyses. More-complex charts would require equation (4.2) to be used.

Further observations from risk signatures or risk dimension signatures

There are many specific observations that describe the dynamics of the risks along each of the predetermined dimensions that relate to the RDS for the ITO exercise. A specific observation that is highlighted, i.e. the extent to which the risk can be 'stretched', identifies the organization's tolerance of risk, or 'risk appetite', along each dimension. Risk appetite is the preference and tolerance for risk of the supplier and/or the buyer organization. An organization's risk appetite is also referred to by the extent to which it tolerates risks as described by performance indicators, operational parameters and process controls. The organization's tolerance for risk or risk appetite is highlighted when the risks are discussed and demonstrated in an illustration of a risk profile.

This risk tolerance can be mapped as an additional RDS plot. It will indicate the extent of risk exposure along each of the dimensions that the organization is prepared to tolerate. The actual RDS then will illustrate areas where this tolerance is either exceeded or is within the limits set. For example, when a customer relationship management (CRM) application is developed by an IT developer for a retail chain, there are significant risks along the technical dimension; there is high risk (level 4) here but low risk on the financial parameter (level 1). The signature clearly identifies 'stress' loads in the area of technology (new, unproven technology). This example is illustrated in Figure 4.3 where the risks and total risk exposure along the technical dimension are high. Coincidentally, the risks in the financial area are lower than those in the others.

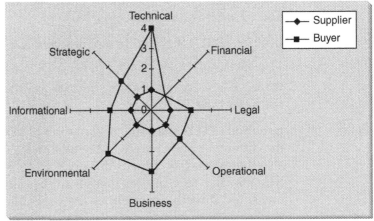

Figure 4.3
Scenario A where the technical risk to the buyer is high (the supplier risk has been held constant for the purposes of illustration)

To reduce the stress loading on technology, perhaps more money can be allocated to additional expertise, to experienced consulting assistance and perhaps also to further investigation in the area of CRM. This increases the finance risk but the risk signature looks more evenly distributed; the overall risk loading is also more evenly distributed.

When more money is spent to 'fix' the technical problem, the risk profile as indicated by the RDS in Figure 4.4, indicates a profile that is much more evenly distributed. The other dimensions can be compared similarly. For example, the interrelationships

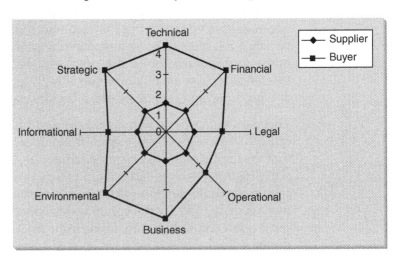

Figure 4.4
Scenario A where some technical risk has been 'traded' for financial risk (the supplier risk has been held constant for the purposes of illustration)

and impact of operations, business and information are reciprocal in nature.

4.3   Additional RDSs and patterns

The risk profiles and patterns also illustrate information on the level of risk exposure or risk severit; risk dimensions for attention; and dimensions that are missing. For example, an acute angle along any single axis could represent a significant variance in risk levels between dimensions, which causes undue stresses to outsourcing agreements for either the buyer or supplier.

Sample RDS patterns and interpretation

An obtuse angle, on the other hand, typically defines a more-balanced risk-sharing profile between risk dimensions (see Figure 4.5). The star and arrowhead topologies have features in common, i.e. have extreme risks along the north–south- and east–west-facing risk dimensions compared to the other shapes. This indicates severe risk exposure at each 'point' or 'tip' compared to the central area of the 'star'.

The circular topology shown demonstrates the 'ideal' risk profile where the magnitude of risk is similar along all the risk dimensions. This indicates some degree of risk sharing and management for the outsourcing arrangement. When risk is drastically reduced along selected risk dimensions, for example arbitrary dimensions C and G along the horizontal axis, a squeezed rectangular shape emerges. The stresses placed on the other risk dimensions would be high. This is discussed further in the following sections.

A circular topology for the buyer indicates even risk sharing between the risk dimensions, and an arrowhead indicates significantly lower risk along two dimensions. When one topology is superimposed on another, the mismatch causes significant strain on the contracting and governance processes necessary to equalize the risk profiles. Even though the buyer would be content, the uneven risk exposure will create a handicapped situation.

Therefore, to summarize, the RDS profile will also allow several characteristics to be monitored and observed. These include the following:

1. An illustration or measure of total risk exposure (by computation).
2. A 'feel' of the areas which are subject to additional or reduced risk (by comparison).

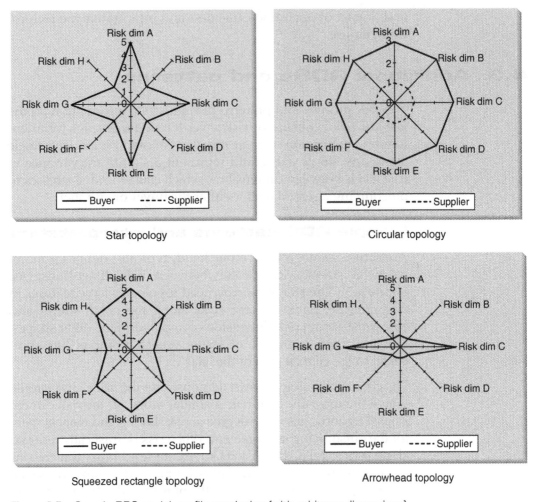

Figure 4.5 Sample RDS or risk profile topologies (with arbitrary dimensions)

3. An understanding of the areas subject to unduly high or low levels of risk and risk exposure (by reviewing the RDS on a stand-alone basis); and
4. An assurance that the 'gut feel' for risks is correct (by careful and detailed observation of the negotiating parties and the environment).

4.4 IT outsourcing (ITO) measurement framework

The intrinsic risks need to be considered in any outsourcing situation. For example, the need to retain the ability to change strategy and options can lead to risks of increases in hidden costs, costs of services and management costs, which are difficult to forecast or budget for. Additional reasons that have been cited include the risk of loss of intellectual property, the risk of loss of competency and the 'lock-in' phenomenon where the contractual obligations impose limitations on both the buyer and the supplier in seeking alternative means to perform the outsourced task. It can be shown, however, that a few key risk areas dominate, i.e. have larger risk exposure than have other risks, in the ITO environment.

Considering multiplicity of risks

To make the measurement of the assortment or multiplicity of risk elements easier, the risks are sorted into groups with similar risk characteristics. IT-related risks have been classified to include elements such as operational failure or lack of reliability (Markus and Tannis, 2000), security breaches, reputation damage to an organization owing to its failure to safeguard the privacy of customer data, and strategic risk (such as adopting a new IT too soon or too late). These risks form the most significant portion of risks in the IT exercise. Risks involved with the IT function in combination with an outsourcing exercise are unique. They are quite different for each area considered separately. In the outsourcing of the IT function within an organization, the complex operations of both the IT function and the outsourcing exercise need to be considered together. The risks in the outsourcing of the IT function are also exacerbated by the fact that IT (and its components) characteristically evolves very rapidly and has very short product life cycles.

Considering contract periods

ITO agreements cover relatively very long periods (many ITO agreements span 5 to 10 years). Implicit in this observation, the products and services that are supplied and used relating to the outsourcing of the IT function also change many times over the period of the outsourcing agreement. By inference then, the inevitable changes in the operating environment (including people, technology, processes and supporting business requirements) become natural catalysts that give rise to an environmental risk consideration. Consequently also, risk effects that are experienced in the ITO exercise are directly related to the organization and its IT policies.

In an ITO exercise these IT risks, together with the risks inherent in an outsourcing exercise, come together and are experienced by both the supplier and buyer of outsourcing services. The effects of ITO risks have been shown (Aubert *et al.*, 1998) along two main measurement metrics, i.e. 'the importance of potential loss' and 'the probability of undesirable outcomes'. The framework for risks built by these researchers allows an assessment of the level of risk exposure for each ITO decision. There is also a group of risks that form the most significant portion of risks in the ITO exercise. Together, the most significant IT project-risks, along with the ITO-risks, form the basis for the most significant measurements of risk exposure that the framework deals with.

Considering buyer and supplier

The information in the frameworks allows a comparison between the elements of risk exposure for both the buyer and supplier organizations. It does not demonstrate, however, the dynamics of the interaction that exists between the causes and effects of the decisions that are made to mitigate the risks. Also, the effects of changes in risk exposure levels are often inter-related. The effects and relationships in this interaction require new methods, tools and frameworks for their observation and measurement. Outsourcing arrangements are partnerships between the buyer and supplier organizations over an agreed period. They constitute alternatives to the more traditional transaction-based contracts, which are usually shorter and defined to deliver specific services or products. An ITO arrangement, for example, may span a period of 10 years or ten financial periods wherein new budgets, strategies and plans will be formulated to balance the forces in a competitive environment.

The risks are often passed from the supplier to the buyer and vice versa (see previous chapter). Risk exposure is also observed to be passed from one risk dimension to another within the virtual confines of either entity. In many examples, the organizations (both buyer and supplier) become increasingly reliant on the structures and, in particular, on the dependencies of a networked environment. As more organizations adopt outsourcing practices, the interconnected systems, processes and people networks increase the inherent risks created in partnership and joint working relationships. Developments in principal-agency theory discussed in the previous section (Chapter 3) have given some insight into the incentive mechanisms used inside organizations, and, by extension, into the role of information and information technology. However, because the same models apply equally well to contracts between organizations, agency theory by itself cannot explain the boundaries of organizations or the relative advantages of different institutional or ownership structures.

4.5 Shifting the 'effects of risk'

One reason why organizations outsource their IT function is to shift some elements of risk from the customer (buyer) to the supplier. The buyer of outsourcing services hopes to transfer away its operational and technical risks by passing them to a supplier organization that will, effectively, take them over and agree to deliver a set of outcomes.

During an ITO exercise, however, actions performed by either the supplier or buyer of outsourcing services can change the nature and severity levels of risk experienced by either party. There are compromises made by both parties in the outsourcing exercise. Anecdotal evidence can be found in examples of ITO failures that have been partly attributed to insufficient focus on an area that was neglected or 'unacceptably exposed' to risk factors. As risks are transferred away, other risk elements appear to enlarge (see examples below). If separate RDS profiles were to be taken for the buyer and the supplier over two different points in time, especially at different stages in the outsourcing exercise, the shifts in risk would become very apparent. An example is illustrated in Chapter 8 in the case study.

Risk-shifts between buyer and supplier

As the risks are shifted from the buyer to the supplier and vice versa, the RDS profiles indicate that each of the risk dimensions also change. This interaction between buyer and supplier actions and the risk exposure can be observed qualitatively. An example to illustrate the risk-shift phenomenon is now discussed. Consider a situation where the amount of money budgeted for use in the purchase of essential backup disks is insufficient or untimely. This means that copies of the 'live' operating data cannot be taken and stored. Operational risk is hence increased because there is no duplicate copy of the 'live' data. Here, an action from the area of finance has affected the area of operations along a sequential chain of events. Financial risk needs to be reduced; costs have to be controlled; insufficient money is allocated for activities which are not urgently required (i.e. purchase of disks for copies); disks for copies hence have not been purchased and copies of the 'live' data not made. These factors cause the operational risks to increase because there is no contingency plan should the data on the computers be destroyed or corrupted by an event like a malicious attack by a computer virus or a natural calamity like a fire. There are no duplicate copies available to replace originals that might be destroyed. In this case, the risks in the area of operations are elevated in an effort to reduce financial exposure and risk. Financial risks have been traded off against operational risks.

Another example of interrelationships between activities and risks is illustrated in the area of contract management. Often contracts are made between the supplier and buyer of outsourcing services at the beginning of the contract, which might only be a few years old. These contracts have a short 'shelf-life', and, unless updated, become quickly outdated because new technology has replaced the old, skills required have changed, and processes and delivery mechanisms are different. Microsoft Corporation's almost ubiquitous Windows operating system for basic personal computers for example, has had major changes on no less than three occasions in the last 5 years, i.e. from Windows 98, Windows Me, and Windows XP. New features and functions often translate into new performance measurement criteria for the supplier of IT services. This may seem trivial at first but when an organization has hundreds of personal computers in its inventory in geographically disparate locations, any exercise to upgrade IT components often becomes a major task and an area of operational risk. As a buyer of outsourced IT services, however, the technical and operational risks appear to have decreased as a result of the deployment of better and more efficient technology, but the legal and operational risks are increased in a complex set of interrelationships.

So what are the implications of these observations on shifting risk? How are the risks in one area traded off against another, if at all? What constitutes an acceptable risk for any one area? What are the levels of risk that each area of the organization can, or should, carry? While heuristics and the cumulative experience that managers of organizations who are involved with the outsourcing of the IT function have applied for years have proven useful in responding to these questions, the dramatic and ever-increasing changes brought about by new components in IT coupled with the increasing scope of outsourcing exercises make this experience an untrustworthy guide.

A typical outsourcing agreement or arrangement often involves neglect of the relationship and interaction between the buyer and supplier organizations. The risk of the buyer organization increases when disagreements emerge about the provision of the outcomes of outsourcing services. Without a systematic analytical approach to the outsourcing decision, the organization may make arbitrary choices on the decision to outsource, based on historic norms, cash flow difficulties, political considerations or misperceptions of the benefit–risk trade-off. Also, given that there is an agency model in operation, many of the activities and risks involved are derived from the fact that people have a tendency to cheat and take advantage of a situation, as articulated in what is known as agency theory (Eisenhardt, 1989). Agency theory explains how to best organize relationships in which one party (the buyer) determines the work which another party (the supplier) undertakes. The theory argues that under conditions of incomplete information and uncertainty as occurs in an ITO environment, agency problems arise.

4.6 Observing risks in an ITO environment

It is understood from the review that while partnership arrangements vary considerably in their operations, from flexibly defined, formal contracts, to loose strategic initiatives, they also include the provision of shared risk and benefits. As observed in Chapter 1 (Figure 1.4) strategic or transformational outsourcing provides for a set of partners who have a considerable stake in the game, and often that means sharing both risk and reward. How is the disproportionate weighting of risk between the supplier and buyer, if any, then quantified? How are the risks of the disproportionate experience levels of the buyer and supplier mitigated?

The phenomenon of winner's curse (Kern *et al.*, 2002), as described below, is the situation where extreme cost cutting is undertaken by the winning supplier based on the risks to supplier when it agrees to enter into the outsourcing contract. What are the risks involved? How are the risks quantified and decisions made?

As this chapter opened by discussing foundational concepts and what has been learned about what works and what does not, as well as the conceptual models for understanding when organizations should and should not outsource, it concludes by focusing on the key area of risks within the ITO environment.

It is simply not possible for this book to attempt to answer all the possible questions posed in an ITO exercise. It recognizes, however, the central theme of risk measurement and management that needs to be addressed, and aims to provide the reader with the appropriate tools and information to be able to manage each individual situation that arises as a separate case. Further, it recognizes that there is a lack of cohesive evidence, supported by any tools or methods, that allows the recognition of risks within the framework of decision-making in an outsourcing exercise. Specifically, the outsourcing of the IT function introduces unique features that add to the complexity of the risks argument.

A series of complex factors including operational, strategic and environmental factors influence risk. In addition, less-predictable human factors, explained through the presence of agency theory as well as observable factors between both the supplier and buyer, affect the behaviour of risks. In order to assess the effect of these complex sets of influences on the risk profile, a tool needs to be developed.

The IT environment is unique and the nature of the outsourcing of the IT function is arguably distinct between industries and also between the operational and business functions that are out-sourced; therefore the application of the concepts of risk needs to be made for each of the projects that the reader is involved with.

There are also two very important observations that arise from the RDS profiles and discussion of risks in the ITO exercise. The first is the notion of the winner's curse which very aptly describes a situation where the winner actually loses because of the bidding framework that is typically used in an ITO scenario. This provides an added reason why the RDS profile is critical for the supplier of ITO services as it will provide both early warning as well as a tool to compute the basic risks that would be encountered in such an activity. The supplier would then be able to assess the impact of increases in risks that exceed its risk tolerance or risk appetite.

The other observation is founded on the agency theory. Agency theory describes the behaviour of people who work with either the buyer or supplier organization. This 'human' behaviour is demonstrated very clearly in the RDS profiles in almost all the risk dimensions. It is possibly the most significant cause of risks within the ITO framework and is described below.

4.7 Winner's curse

Very often, in search of cost savings, the buyer drives the supplier's prices down, resulting in winner's curse (which is also a loss for the buyer as services deteriorate in compensation). Alternatively the process is abandoned because the costs of providing the services are too high.

The tender process described is quite similar to a bidding or auction process where the lowest price (not the highest) is sought by the buyer of outsourcing services. Acceptance of a bid is often based on the information provided by the buyer. Failure to incorporate relevant and correct information into the bidding strategy can lead to excessively low bids and subsequent losses. Each bidder then works through a series of decisions to price the outsourcing services. As information is not always forthcoming, the risk of the winner paying more, on average, than the prize is worth, is something found to happen quite often in practice. This series of actions leads to the 'winner's curse' phenomenon. It occurs in normal auctions, in which the auctioneer is the seller or represents the seller and the bidders are the buyers, who have evaluated the object(s) sold.

The incidence of this phenomenon has been increasing with the recent development of business-to-business (B2B) exchanges and on-line auctions. In all sorts of markets, a winner's curse can have consequences for several parties, over months or even years. In such circumstances, auctions themselves may well be better conceived as relationship-building exercises rather than one-off bids.

The theory of auctions would suggest that the winner's curse is asymmetric, i.e. it only affects the supplier or the winning bid. In this case however, the winner's curse in a procurement auction of ITO contracts and its impact on and consequences for the relationship between the customer and the winning bidder starts the interplay of risk-shifting. The supplier winning a 'cursed' deal may well cut losses by supplying lower-quality products or services to the customer. Then the buyer, winning what turns out to be a cursed deal, may well drive a much harder bargain in terms of service guarantee rather than price. The upshot may be that the buyer removes the offending supplier from its supplier listing.

Inexperienced suppliers tend to make unrealistic bids. Other suppliers make bidding promises to 'buy' the contract. Subsequently however, the risks on not being able to recover their tendering, business, and operational costs could become significant problems. The risk therefore has shifted back from the buyer to the supplier.

In an effort to recover their costs, the suppliers would either attempt to offer additional services from their portfolio of technology capabilities, service management, and consultancy services over the life of the contract or, under pressure, to make sufficient margins in unfavourable circumstances and trade-offs in the quality of service. The risk, hence, is shifted back from the supplier to the buyer. Case studies confirm that when a supplier seeks to decrease its costs, this can result in decreases in service quality and additional costs for the client.

Further, the supplier's disproportionate concern for keeping its costs down could lead to inflexibility in the interpretation of the contract, and subsequently lead to adversarial relationships. Operational performance and the client–buyer relationship will receive less attention and suffer; the success and effectiveness of the operations and outsourcing relationship will be compromised. The focus of the supplier will be primarily on recovering costs, and not on developing and maintaining the relationship and mutual objectives.

The process wherein suppliers are asked to bid in an 'auction' provides a mechanism whereby the procurement of ITO services from lowest supplier induces the suppliers to disclose their privately known cost structures. As illustrated earlier, the auction mechanism enables the buyer and supplier to match services and goods with an optimal price, especially in this instance where a standard market price is unavailable. While a discussion on auction mechanisms and variations in auction designs are not dealt with here, the risk profile identifies the tolerance limits for both the supplier and the buyer organizations as input into the design for auction mechanisms. Costs and the related financial risks are important factors for a business organization and the auction allows it to procure services at more competitive prices. In addition, 'market solutions are viable for reducing differences in information and hidden action when these differences are limited to a single dimension or when intermediaries exist to disseminate credible information regarding counterparty behaviour'. The supplier governance procedures are constructed by the organization to mitigate informational and legal risks. The RDS, once again, reveals this to the managers at an early stage in both supplier and buyer organizations if the tool is used.

4.8 Agency theory

Agency theory provides a background to the interaction and motivation of the supplier and buyer of outsourcing services. Opportunism, or the tendency to cheat as a means to gain advantage, is an inherent characteristic of many relationships where there is an agent and 'buyer'. In the outsourcing relationship, this leads the supplier to adopt opportunistic behaviour whenever the chance arises, to its own benefit. The assumption is the tendency of the supplier to behave in this way despite the existence of moral and social norms as well as the constant risk of prosecution. Opportunism in turn manifests in terms of moral hazard, adverse selection, and imperfect commitment.

An essential area in the discussion of the main relationship risks in an ITO scenario is the relationship itself, from the viewpoint of agency theory. This applies to both participants (the buyer and the supplier) within the ITO scenario. Agency theory mentioned earlier postulates that because people are self-interested, they will have conflicts of interests over at least some issues. This occurs any time they attempt to engage in co-operative endeavours. Some of the salient points of the behaviours that manifest are summarized in Figure 4.6.

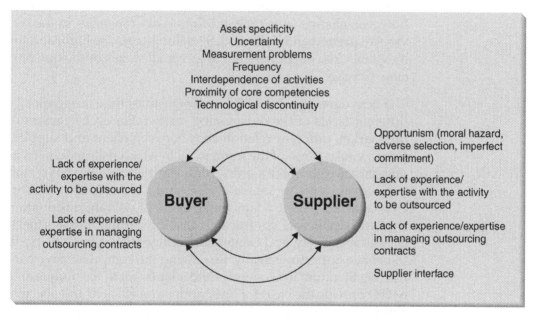

Figure 4.6   IT outsourcing risk factors between buyer and supplier (Tho, 2003)

Moral hazard arises as a consequence of the buyer not being able to accurately monitor the activities of the supplier without incurring prohibitive costs. The buyer hence cannot easily determine whether a problem is the result of negligence on the part of its supplier or to an unforeseeable event. This is a significant risk factor borne by the buyer, as the supplier has the 'excuse' that poor performance is beyond its control. This leads to an increased risk for the buyer over the supplier. The supplier can choose to assign his best staff to a project or use his most inexperienced teams without a thorough background check on every person placed on a project at every point in time. The existence of the latter scenario is difficult to detect, but it may manifest itself in decreased reliability, excessive cost or project delays.

It can also manifest itself as a consequence of the supplier not being able to monitor the buyer. A buyer of outsourcing services may undertake hidden investments even before the contract is signed. Many outsourcing agreements are based on an initial benchmarking period where actual cost is measured, and the supplier is given a bonus for cost reduction. Buyers excessively invest in cost reduction before contract initiation in order to limit supplier bonuses from cost de-escalation clauses.

Given the contractual nature of outsourcing, the service quality is not as flexible as would be the case if the services were to be delivered without the outsourcing services. These services, however, change over time, leading to discrepancies in the services requested and delivered. Switching-costs are high, and the inevitable loss of competence arises at all stages of the outsourcing exercise.

The heterogeneity of the ITO market justifies the examination of different facets of the outsourcing market. For each segment of the market, different relationships between client and supplier form a vital portion of the framework in which risks in this environment are examined. Contractual risks between the buyer and supplier are a prime source of risks and a factor in the outsourcing decision. The fundamental drivers of risk are information asymmetries before contracting, inability to monitor partners' actions accurately, and exogenous changes that allow one party to behave opportunistically. Reviewing the comprehensive contracting literature in economics and adapting it to the unique area of ITO provide the basis for prescriptions on efficient and effective contractual arrangements. These prescriptions are in the form both of governance structures that emphasize the importance of ownership of critical assets and of contractual remedies to provide sufficient incentives to align parties' interests.

If all actions that affect the value of a relationship are fully observable and verifiable, an outsourced contract is based on a documented set of agreed requirements and the payments contingent on completing them. Incentive payments are then necessary to align interests between the buyer and supplier. Much of the economics of the agreement is about the incentive systems and how they perform under different conditions.

Another critical economic issue in an outsourcing contract is risk sharing. Both the buyer and supplier may have different preferences for risk, which generates opportunities for gains in the contract exercise. As parties become increasingly risk averse, so too can the cost of very highly attractive contracts become expensive because of the high-risk premium required.

Mutually unobservable behaviour may lead to inter-organizational problems associated with imperfect commitment. This frequently manifests itself through the problem of 'double-sided moral hazard' or mutual shirking.

'Adverse selection' arises when the buyer has difficulty choosing a supplier based on a given set of characteristics. Information asymmetries can be so severe that markets for certain goods can completely disappear or only low-quality goods become available for purchase. The appearance of selection errors that may result from an exaggeration of the facts by the supplier is common and is known as 'hubris' or 'over-exuberance'. This expectation gap between the supplier's performance at the time of selection and performance of work is a risk borne by the buyer.

When performance is not to the level expected and disputes occur, both buyers and suppliers may not honour commitments that were made at the time of contract agreement for reasons of changed circumstances. Imperfect commitment and unclear and/or incomplete contracts are often used as reasons. Again, the buyer carries significantly more risk, given that the ultimate responsibility originated with and still resides with the buyer.

This risk from an inexperienced buyer could be to severely underestimate transition and management costs. This puts the buyer organization at risk and vulnerable to the supplier's opportunistic behaviour. On the other hand, the people resources taken over by the supplier from the buyer to manage legacy systems may not carry over sufficient expertise to enable the management of newer systems. The inexperience of the buyer of outsourcing services in the area of contract and supplier management also introduces a risk, particularly in the area where a relationship exists between the buyer and a wide range of suppliers that provide services for a prime supplier. The buyer ultimately carries the risks of diluted responsibility and opportunism.

The other risk factors relate to the transactions themselves. Asset specificity is the degree to which an asset can be reused once the supplier takes over operations, i.e. the extent to which its value needs to be sacrificed. Neither the buyer nor the supplier can predict with enough certainty the activities to be performed in the agreement. This is particularly true in the area of IT management where the complex set of applications, hardware, networks and new technology is thrown into the mix constantly. This is aggravated by the fact that businesses are constantly challenged to use this 'IT mix' to enable the proper functioning of core business strategy and operations. Unclear business objectives cannot drive IT development. Subsequently also, IT cannot enable the appropriate business functions to deliver business objectives, which remain ambiguous. For example, electronic ticketing has been seen as a strategic business enabler for competitive advantage. In a more remote setting, however, access to the Internet is restricted to a section of the community as a result of poor communications and social profile. Even if IT systems were able to deliver Internet ticketing successfully, the strategy would still fail as a result of an ambiguous business objective.

Measuring the value of the activities, processes and items exchanged is therefore also a challenge. The frequency of activities needs to be understood. It is beneficial to carry the risks associated with investments or uncertainty rather than invest in transactions that only occur once. Outsourcing interdependent activities within the IT function already causes serious difficulties. When IT is used to enable the running of business functions, this risk factor is compounded. For example, disputation over poor response time would then need to be attributed to more than one system, and ownership would be difficult to identify. Further, a risk factor arises if the supplier does not provide the latest technology that enables the buyer organization to maintain competitive advantage over its competitors.

A risk factor that is often highlighted and often not satisfactorily investigated is when the core competence of a buyer organization is outsourced. The buyer risks that the suppliers could either take it over in its own market space, or move in directions different from the ones the buyer might take strategically. Outsourcing an activity at the core of the organization could be potentially disruptive to the learning capabilities of its staff and reduce its overall competitiveness.

The governance structures set up during an outsourcing arrangement, the contracts, and the informal arrangements created to reduce conflict, to govern relations, and to increase the extent of co-operation and benefits, will provide the framework of controls in the buyer's arsenal to mitigate the 'human' risks presented in an outsourcing agreement. A contract in itself, however, is also an area of risk exposure. The same contract will induce changes in behaviour and methods used, and hence also reduce the losses incurred associated with undesirable outcomes or reduce the probability of occurrences of such outcomes.

Amendments to the outsourcing contract are routine, either because the buyer organization's needs are changing, or because most contracts are indeed incomplete. As a result, many suppliers have used high charges. New services or changes are then renegotiated for services rendered. The uneven risk profile is skewed against the buyer.

A lock-in situation often results from specific investments that were made by the supplier when the contract was first signed. At contract renewal time, if no other supplier is ready to make specific investments, the client has no alternative but to continue its relationship with the current supplier. The supplier can then increase its fees because of this lack of an alternative. The lock-in situation is more likely to occur in an industry where there are specialized IT requirements (buyer organizations for example) and there are only a small number of suppliers that are capable of managing the IT function. When the time comes to renew the contract, the buyer organization will not have many alternatives to consider. The supplier can then almost dictate the conditions of the contract and the risks to the buyer are escalated.

Service quality and service costs are two major issues in ITO. The literature shows examples of degraded service levels resulting from outsourcing, including poor response time, poor turn-around time, late software updates and applications that do not meet requirements. Along with service degradation, service costs rise. This imposes a more significant risk on the buyer than on the supplier of outsourcing services. Financial penalties are often imposed for non-compliance with service quality arrangements. These contracts, however, also impose a formidable resource requirement for measurement and governance. This imperfection, discussed earlier, does not help to mitigate this risk.

People- or resource-risks are also higher for the buyer compared with the supplier. After an outsourcing agreement is reached, often very few IT resources or little expertise remains in the buyer organization. This creates an initially advantageous cost position. It can, however, also be viewed as dangerous, since the organization will have lost its ability to use IT efficiently and effectively, and will remain dependent on an external supplier. Again, the risk profile is highly skewed against the buyer.

Given that the RDS profiles measure the risk exposure value and allow the managers in the ITO exercise to understand the risks dynamics, the next chapter provides some insight into the observed relationship between risk dimensions that is evident when the RDS is used. It is observed that the risk dimensions are interrelated to a significant extent. This observation also reveals an opportunity that can be exploited in order to mitigate risks, as explained in Section III (Mitigating (& managing) risks in IT outsourcing), the final component of the MUM method proposed earlier.

Risk interaction in IT outsourcing

Managers who work with IT outsourcing (ITO) without using the risk dimension signature (RDS) tool or similar instrument described in the previous section, are often confronted with the predicament of having to rely on instinct and 'gut feel' for the impending risks. Some organizations will have a higher propensity for risk than others, and form a group of early adopters of the ITO concept. These organizations are not able to reap the maximum benefit of ITO as risk diminishes the benefits accruing to the ITO participants. There is, therefore, significant advantage to be gained from understanding the workings of the RDS and its implementation in this environment.

5.1 Interaction between supplier and buyer in IT outsourcing

Risks are transferred via instruments like legal contracts and process changes between the supplier and buyer of outsourcing services, and vice versa, on multiple occasions during the term of an outsourcing agreement. This extends the original observation in this area on the shifting risks from the buyer to the supplier in the operations dimension. When the identified risks are tracked between the pair of stakeholders in a typical ITO exercise, an obvious 'to-ing' and 'fro-ing' of risk between the buyer and supplier is observed along several sets of risks. Importantly, however, in a 'musical chairs' fashion, the party left with the risk when the undesirable event occurs is stuck with the consequences. Supplier organizations experience a set of risks that are adopted from the buyer, and vice versa. A reasonable conclusion hence could be that, in an outsourcing arrangement, there are no exclusive supplier or buyer risks, merely risks that are shared or remain with one party temporarily (then passed on to the other party).

The paradox effect

There is also a 'paradox effect' that is observed. For example, when organizations outsource to save money, they often get more worried about being exploited on cost; when they outsource to improve service, they fear it may deteriorate; and when they outsource to avoid the hassle of management, they still need to control.

The risks are either shared between the supplier and buyer through a series of agreements and activities or passed between risk sets or types in the individual organizational risk-landscape. The objective of the tool proposed is to assist in illustrating and identifying these risk sets and then determining the level of risks that can be tolerated at any single point in time. It allows the appropriate decisions and mitigating activities to be implemented early, in order to avoid often unbearable consequences.

Assume an organization has made the decision to outsource its IT function to derive competitive advantage in its market space and improve operations and performance. Further assume that there are suppliers that have sufficient economies of scale and superior IT management practices to deliver improved services at a lower price, and that the resulting savings are those that the client will benefit from.

A typical outsourcing selection process exists where a list of suppliers is created through advertising for an ITO project. Suppliers are invited to make submissions. They are then short-listed through a process where likely suppliers are identified based on a set of requirements. Once short-listed, suppliers are issued with a Request For Information (RFI) document that outlines the buyer's objectives, services, assets, transfers, and issues of relevance to the outsourcing exercise. Suppliers respond by matching the buyer's expectations with their own capabilities, track record, reference sites, and associated information. Those selected are then 'invited to tender' and issued a Request For Proposal (RFP) or Request For Tender (RFT). The process may differ slightly as a result of probity and procurement regulations often already set out in the buyer's corporate policies.

A supplier would likely undertake opportunistic behaviour, seeking to reduce its own operational costs, often at the expense of the client. Social actors will behave opportunistically if it is advantageous for them to do so. This opportunism denotes the capability and willingness of organizations to pursue their own interests at the expense of partners by withholding, for example, information.

Relationship dynamics between buyer and supplier

The selection process for a suitable supplier takes on the form of an auction where several suppliers are invited to tender for the outsourcing activity. As in an auction situation however, when the winner of the auction or bidding event systematically bids above the actual value of the objects or service, the bidder incurs losses. The suppliers are 'squeezed' to provide the lowest prices. The difficulty in such bidding circumstances is to select those suppliers that offer the best deal. There is little or no differentiation between suppliers that is obvious during the selection process. Selection of the supplier hence tends to be based on what cost efficiencies suppliers can deliver.

The interplay of winning and losing scenarios is illustrated in Figure 5.1 where the ideal scenario would be for the buyer to obtain the best service delivery from the supplier, who in turn must be paid a 'correct' price.

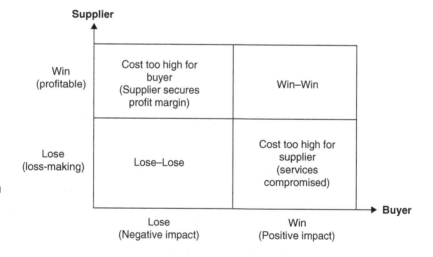

Figure 5.1
Interaction between supplier and buyer in the selection process

5.2 Implications of relationship for risk

To derive a win–win situation (Figure 5.1), the relative risks of the 'supplier' and the 'buyer' of services in the outsourcing of the IT function are expected to be shared almost equally. This is not the case. While identifiable operational risks are transferred to the supplier, there are significant risks and inherent business risks that remain with the buyer. In addition to this, the risks associated with the relationship make the risk scenario or profile often too difficult to bear.

Interplay between buyer and supplier RDSs

That the buyer carries a larger RDS or risk profile in comparison with the supplier needs to be recognized by both sides in order to derive a synergistic relationship. The emergence of partnership or alliance arrangements as alternatives to the formerly more popular transaction-based contracts[1] indicates a shift to closer interactions between buyer and supplier. While partnership arrangements vary considerably in their operations, from flexibly defined, formal contacts, to loose strategic initiatives, they also include the provision of shared risk and benefits. Transformational outsourcing provides for a set of partners who have a considerable stake in the game, and often that means sharing both risk and reward.

The need for successful outsourcing decisions and contractual arrangements in an ITO deal involves the understanding and management of risks inherent in the deal. Risk assessment and risk management are consequently critical contributors to the success and/or failure of an ITO venture. The understanding of the relative risk profile or signature between the buyer and supplier of services will enable appropriate action to be taken to manage the relationship.

While the direct financial benefits[2], in terms of cost reduction, are a major driver to divest the organization's 'non-core activities', there is a clear move to the outsourcing of products and/or services in consideration of scale and costs, that is, financial considerations. The risk, however, is often not qualified and can result in losses not recognized in an organization's financial statements. This can be, however, qualitatively measured.

The outsourcing decision ultimately breaks down into a cost–benefit trade-off. Again, the important benefits that the organization achieves when outsourcing include economies of scale, scope and specialization. To achieve these benefits, it incurs costs such as supplier organization search, negotiations, and legal fees to establish the relationships. 'Outsourcing can ease many maladies – people shortages, skills gaps, and over-ambitious corporate plans. But increasingly, it can also improve your chance of seeing the inside of a courtroom' (Goodridge, 2001). These costs, however, are often dwarfed by contractual risks associated with inefficient contracts, owing to differences in information

---

[1] Usually a shorter and more tightly defined contract arrangement
[2] Often over a period of (5) to 10 years

between the parties (asymmetric information), inability to observe actions comprehensively; and the inherent incompleteness of IT contracts. These risks are often driven by the large uncertainty surrounding IT investments, parties' inherent risk aversion and bounded rationality.

Sharing of risks between buyer and supplier

When the buyer's operational risks are being shared with the supplier, this is often perceived as an advantage to the buyer. This is because the resources now required to support risk mitigation for the buyer are reduced (as they are now shared with the supplier). Along with the sharing of operations risk, the responsibility for recovery from adverse activities as a result of the risk is also shared. These advantages provide support for the argument for outsourcing. There are a number of critical risks of ITO, including cost increases, management issues, service failures, loss of expertise and negative business impacts, including loss of innovation. Finally, there are questions as to whether the potential benefits of outsourcing offset the management risks that it introduces.

If just the buyer side of the agreement is observed, then the operational risks are qualitatively and arguably reduced. The other risks, including financial risk, risk on reliance of the supplier and environmental risks such as the catastrophic risk of business failure as a result of failure by the supplier to deliver, are arguably increased. The interplay between the risks and severity of risks along each of these dimensions or risk sets appears to take on several characteristics including the ability to trade off one for the other and interdependence. Importantly also however, the risks appear also to be able to be managed as a result of certain sets of actions taken by the contracting organizations in the risks landscape.

5.3 Sharing risks within one organization, between value activities

Much has been said in the literature about the linkages within the organization value chain regarding the sharing of risks. The value chain is a concept introduced by Michael Porter (1985), where the organizational activities, both primary and support, are grouped into various categories. Porter identified the linkages between value activities that are interdependent and that provide the organization with competitive advantage through cost or functional differentiation. By extrapolation, the linkages still exist for the risks involved when one of the major support activities like technology is intentionally removed for performance by an external party. By implication, then, the risk profiles of the related value activities also change. The profiling graph provides another analytical tool to monitor this change.

The value activities are linked through intricate relationships. For example, the implementation of a computerized organization resource planning (ERP) application tool will affect primary activities such as supply chain activities, logistics within and external to the organization and, finally, the complete customer experience. This is an anecdotal generalization but is founded on many examples in the literature that can provide empirical evidence. A complete analysis is outwith the scope of this book. The point that needs to be emphasized, however, is that the information gained through the use of technology is fundamental to exploiting value linkages. The downstream effect of this exploitation of technology means that the risks are also shared and spread between the activities in the value chain.

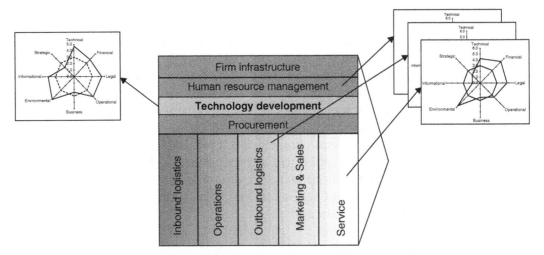

Figure 5.2 Example illustration of risk profiles in interdependent value activities in the organizational value chain (value chain adapted from Porter, 1985)

Risk signature/RDS – supplier

By focusing on the competence areas that are essential to the formation of competitive advantage through product innovation, marketing, and brand development, organizations become reliant on specialized suppliers for providing best-in-class production services to quickly reap value from innovations and spread risk at the same time.

This in itself is a risk that needs at least to be understood to exist and then managed in order to avoid unforeseen and often surprising events that could result in disastrous consequences. A rather straightforward example is when a buyer relies 'blindly' on selected equipment (assets) and specialist services of an outsourcing services supplier who in turn now chooses to raise the prices for its services. There are few choices open to the buyer if this event were not planned for and mitigated either through a contract, through a multi-supplier strategy or even through rigorous governance processes.

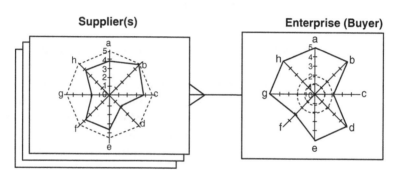

Figure 5.3 A one-to-many relationship between the buyer organization and its supplier(s) of outsourcing services as a strategy to mitigate operational risk of dependence

Risk signature/RDS – buyer

Using a similar risk of reliance on an organization (see above), the supplier organization would invest in selected equipment (assets) and specialist skills to provide the relevant services. This increases its risk if the single buyer were to terminate the outsourcing agreement prematurely. With the right mix of capabilities however, a supplier could reduce its business risk through structuring a multiple customer and/or multiple business profile.

In a typical IT support function, modularization of functions helps suppliers to reduce the degree of asset specificity while maintaining the capability to offer customized services. Having such capabilities, a supplier could further expand its customer base and serve new application areas.

Suppliers, then, are able to ramp output up and down according to changes in demand. Similarly, suppliers are able to achieve relatively stable demand profiles, high capacity utilization rates, and low costs by pooling demand from a large number of customers (buyer organizations) if process technology depends

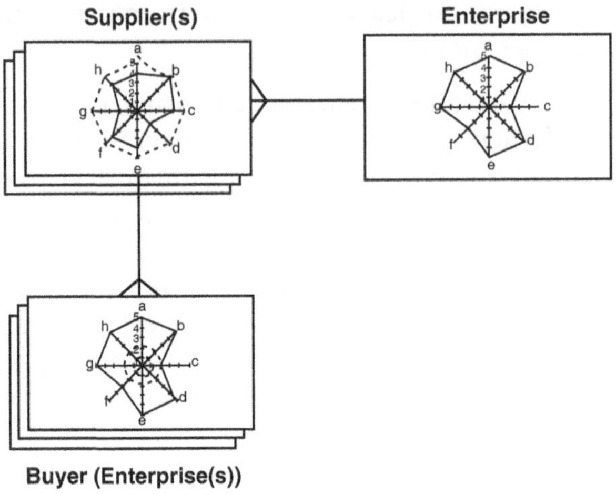

Supplier(s)

Enterprise

Figure 5.4

A reversed relationship where a supplier's risk profile changes in line with its development of multiple relationships with many organizations/IT outsourcing projects

Buyer (Enterprise(s))

not on specific assets, but on generic assets, assets that are widely applicable to the entire customer pool, and suppliers have the capacity to identify and meet the complex requirements of multiple customers and transform that data into a format usable by their generic processes. With the commoditization of IT equipment, processes and techniques, more supplier organizations are finding outsourcing a lucrative business.

To graphically illustrate risk or the negative outcomes, the dimensions of risk to be illustrated are technical, financial, legal, operational, business, environmental, informational and strategic. The loss due to an undesirable outcome can be approximated either via quantitative analysis[3] or via qualitative assessment of the organizational impact of each negative outcome.

5.4 Tolerance for risk exposure (risk appetite)

An outsourcing contract represents a long-term partnership (possibly over 5 years) where the constantly changing business environment and conditions are managed through a governance structure. Both the buyer and supplier [or external services provider (ESP)] has different preferences and tolerance for risk, also described as the 'risk appetite'. The risk premiums required and costs for appropriate risk mitigation activities that need to be factored into the total project costs will differ given

---

[3] For instance, by evaluating the amount of sales lost due to disruption of service to customers

the individual project characteristics and the appetite for risk shown by the contracting organizations.

Risks indicate decision limits in an outsourcing context. The tolerance for risk or risk appetite for uncertainty varies from one organization to another; hence it is important that, first, the levels of tolerance are determined and the risk levels are then managed within these boundaries. For example, risk aversion has paid off for many organizations in an increasingly complex business environment as organizations seek to avoid risks rather than profit from them. As a result, they often overlook the highest-value IT initiatives while spending money on safer but less valuable ideas. To what extent can these organizations, however, tolerate the levels of risk or uncertainty? To remain competitive, organizations need to weigh the 'safety' current capabilities and assets against risks and 'dangers' of increased efficiency and cost-cutting. It is not easy continually to change, as this requires a significant amount of energy, courage and innovative use of new tools.

The RDS proposed earlier is a method to identify and present the multidimensional nature of risk that will enable subsequent understanding of its nature and the forces that either magnify or reduce risk. It is important for management to take a more proactive role in the understanding of risk and its subsequent mitigation.

The elements of risk exposure and risk appetite of the buyer and supplier are also contributory factors. Here, a project with shorter payback period is considered better because of the lower perceived risks. The internal rate of return (IRR) of the ITO project is focused on the stream of the future cash flows and is not impacted by the cost of capital. If the cost of capital equals the IRR there will be no financial benefit from investing in the exercise. Therefore, IRR effectively creates a ceiling for the cost of capital as an example of one component that contributes to the financial risk appetite of the buyer organization. In a separate risk dimension, the IRR is related to the level of operational risk experienced. Generally, the higher the operational risk, the higher the IRR. The IRR, however, reaches a stage where the increase in IRR is no longer acceptable or has exceeded the organization's appetite for risk given the risk levels that are experienced (see Figure 5.5).

In the example used for the illustration of this concept (see Figure 5.5) it is arbitrarily assumed a Level 4 risk is the maximum reasonable exposure to a dimension of risk for, say, the technical

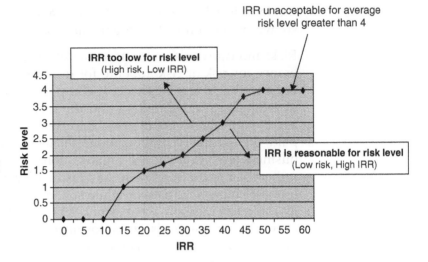

Figure 5.5
A reasonable risk tolerance/exposure level could be a measure of financial internal rate of return (IRR) (example with arbitrary data for illustration only)

dimension. The IRR estimated would then be about 45%. Should the risk exposure decrease, in this example the IRR would also decline. If the supplier were prepared to take risk exposure up to an arbitrary level of 4, then it would need to be prepared to estimate its financial gains for such a risk exposure before agreeing to perform the outsourced function. Another way of reviewing the 'make or buy' decision entails estimating that the expected economic loss (transaction costs and contractual risks), given optimal contractual risk mitigation that can result from an outsourcing contract, exceeds the expected economic gains (difference in production costs). So long as the risks associated with the outsourcing of any single activity do not have expected losses that exceed the expected gains, then, on average, the organization's portfolio of activities should be economically neutral.

5.5 Mapping the risk signature

If arbitrary risk dimensions are then taken in the areas of risk, namely strategic, technical, financial, legal, operational, business (overall performance), environmental (business interaction) and informational (access), one view of risk is fairly well represented. To measure risk sensitivity, a Likert scale on a multidimensional, numeric, empirical index of 0 to 5 is used where 0 represents zero risk and 5, very significant risk. The risk signature (sample in Figure 5.6) can then be used to identify risk type, risk exposure and mix of risks for the organization at that point in time.

Empirical information is available from risk strategies and planning documents. However, this methodology does not provide

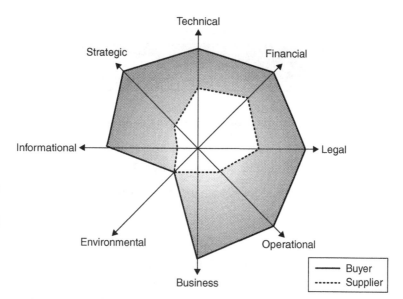

Figure 5.6

The risk profiles of a typical supplier and buyer of outsourcing services show a high skew toward the supplier (lower risk)

precise measurements. The critical information derived represents relative weightings of the risk in the key dimensions identified. The difference between the risk profile of the supplier versus that of the buyer is already visible from a plot of relative weight differences on each of the identified dimensions. The resultant risk signature for the example used in this book is illustrated in Figure 5.6.

A version of the risk landscape would appear as a risk 'signature' for the buyer of outsourcing services. Similarly the risk signature for the supplier could be mapped. What is observed here is that the signature for the buyer is relatively larger than that for the supplier in relation to risk areas that need to be considered. A larger area denotes either a higher probability of risk or a higher loss as a result of the risk experienced. Importantly however, the risk signatures paint a picture of the relative risks along the risk dimensions, allowing for subsequent analysis and management.

5.6 Evaluation dimensions

The data for the supporting dimensions will be derived from the supplier proposals and the organization's executives. The preparation of the weighting criteria would, however, need to be accomplished as part of the development of the assessment tool. The weights applied to the different evaluation elements needed to be reasonable and applicable to the organization, its industrial sector and the IT function.

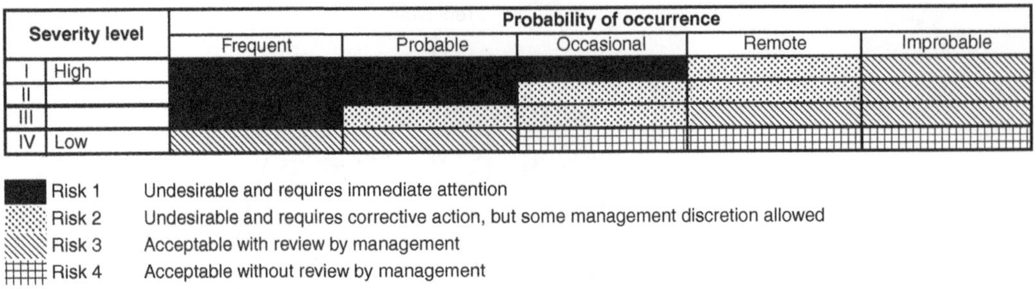

Severity level		Probability of occurrence				
		Frequent	Probable	Occasional	Remote	Improbable
I	High					
II						
III						
IV	Low					

	Risk 1	Undesirable and requires immediate attention
	Risk 2	Undesirable and requires corrective action, but some management discretion allowed
	Risk 3	Acceptable with review by management
	Risk 4	Acceptable without review by management

Source: US Government Accounting Office, 'Information Security Assessment – Practices of Leading Organizations', June 1999

Figure 5.7 The risk tolerance levels from the relationship between the probability of occurrence and severity levels

In Figure 5.7, there are four risk types that have been highlighted for the simplicity of illustration. The resultant matrix when the probability of occurrence (likelihood) is mapped against the severity level (potential impact) defines the organization's risk portfolio (US Government Accounting Office, 1999). What it reveals also is the risk tolerance boundary for the organization. This imaginary boundary lies roughly at the border between risk 2 and risk 3. This concept can then be transposed to the risk profile where all the risk exposure elements are already plotted.

The potential impact on the business would logically form the weighting for the evaluation items. This is also proportional to the risk exposure. The revised approach takes into account the proposed methodology already used in industry.

The dimensions for measurement would also need to be considered. Given the objectives of the outsourcing exercise for the organization, the basic outsourcing services as well as the business transformation work need to be compiled to show the benefits that would accrue from this exercise. The basic outsourcing of the IT function would derive from infrastructure (e.g. hardware, operating systems and databases) and applications (software that perform business functions). The additional value that is sought after, however, lies in the transformation of the organization through the best practices delivered by the (world class) supplier. The transformation practices would be viewed from a systems and business integration perspective. Systems integration would deliver both the traditional services (including familiarity and ability to deliver the infrastructure to operate the business) and new directions (including new architecture for IT components, processes and functions). The business integration advantage would come from the supplier's understanding of the organization's business and business process re-engineering skills.

5.7 Analysing risk with the RDS

The analogy of a risk landscape alluded to in this chapter represents the rich mix of risk dimensions assembled to show the interaction of risk exposure experienced by both the supplier and buyer of ITO services.

As discussed earlier, the RDS is based on various risk analysis frameworks. These risk analysis framework methods are constructed from the measurement of loss and the probability of loss.

The grouping of risks along risk dimensions provides a stage on which risks of a similar nature can be brought together. As was discussed earlier, this implies that the impact of minor variations in measurement as a result of uncertainties in probability of loss magnitudes will be reduced.

With the ability to group risks, the RDS is formulated to illustrate the various dimensions in which risks become manifest in the ITO exercise. The variety of components of IT, the rapid changes in the nature of each component, and the role of the IT function is accommodated because the RDS can be reused when required. Specific areas from the outsourcing of the IT function can be researched and this allows for comparison between risk dimensions.

The information from the RDS is qualitatively illustrated and key features include:

- limits of risk or risk tolerance that can be borne by the organization;
- relative severity of risks between the one stakeholder and another;
- areas where risk dimensions can be 'traded' for another;
- mix of risks and areas of high risk stress (unacceptable risk areas);
- important risk dimensions (as defined by the organization).

Risk profile snapshots at two different points in time reveal information on the effects on risks to the organization along separate dimensions as a result of these actions. The iterative process then continues and becomes an input into the risk assessment methodology, defined in the following chapters, where the concepts and the tool are tested. Importantly also, the risk profile also allows the organization's ITO governance team to steer the activities in outsourcing knowing the stresses on the risk profile relative to these risk dimensions.

It is expected that various nuances and hues on the risk landscape are discernible from the details in the case study (see Chapter 8), giving rise to points of contention. This, however, should not distract attention from the main objective of the exercise, which is to observe possible interaction between risk dimensions that arise in the outsourcing of the IT function. The use of the eight risk dimensions in Figure 3.8 needs to be verified and substantiated each time the RDS is applied.

The RDS described in the previous two chapters is a tool developed specifically for the purpose of examining risks in the ITO environment and examining risk profiles, as described earlier. The RDS was introduced in Chapter 3 to be used as the primary tool for observation of changes in risk profiles. These changes can be measured and observed by applying the RDS at specific times during the ITO exercise.

The patterns portrayed by the risk profile in the previous chapter show risk exposure characteristics including the abnormally high (peaks) or low (troughs) risks encountered at particular points in time. As the set of interrelationships change over time, the mix of risk exposure elements and their relative 'weights' along each of the risk dimensions are also observed to change. The RDS illustrates risks along multiple dimensions and then qualitatively describes the relationships between the risk dimensions that arise in the outsourcing of the IT function. This is done by comparing two versions of the RDS for the same ITO exercise using the same parameters, which change because of events that have occurred in between each recording. During an ITO exercise, the RDS tool can then be used to illustrate the risk profiles that will verify the objectives stated at the start of the book.

The most significant changes in the risk signature are expected to occur when there are new activities or significant changes made to existing processes that occur during the course of the outsourcing exercise. The changes in the RDS profile will demonstrate and validate previous observations and hypotheses on risk sharing and risk transfer between the buyer and supplier. The changes in the risk exposure along each of the risk elements (grouped by risk dimension) are recorded in the RDS illustration; observations of changes in the risk patterns over time show the existence of relationships between the risk dimensions.

When changes are made via programmed activities, risks in the risk dimensions also change. The patterns of risk signature and the size of the total risk exposure throughout the outsourcing exercise are observed to remain constant. The risk exposure values are observed to change within an organization as the nature and use of the IT function change (owing to changes in the profile of the IT components, people or processes). The conclusion is that there exists a set of interrelationships between actions and the effects of these actions that influence the risks along key risk dimensions, so keeping the total risk exposure for the exercise constant.

For illustrative purposes, the buyer and supplier have been assigned arbitrary risk exposure levels of 6 and 5 respectively in Figure 5.8. In the equally spaced, octagonally shaped RDS example, equal risk exposure on all eight risk dimensions is illustrated. The total risk that the buyer is exposed to is larger than that of the supplier.

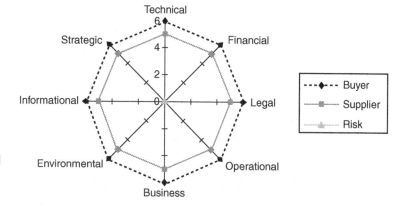

Figure 5.8
Risk levels for both buyer and supplier RDSs indicate equal risks along all dimensions

The risk signature patterns that take shape then provide visual clues to the relationships between the various risk categories or dimensions. For example, an octagonal (almost circular) RDS in Figure 5.8 represents equal risk levels in all dimensions and a protrusion from this circle would represent a point of stress, where the risk is higher than in any other dimension.

The choices made by either the buyer or supplier of ITO services then influence the effects of risks directly; they also indirectly influence the shape of the risk signature along the risk dimensions, forming new risk dimension signatures (RDSs). For example, the risk exposure values are illustrated according to the characteristics of risks along the eight dimensions that are relevant to the outsourcing exercise for the case study (see Chapter 8).

Empirical measurement

As this tool is empirically based, detailed observation of risks within the ITO environment will need to be collected and presented. Risk exposure values for any ITO activity are influenced by a very complex set of factors. Environmental factors such as organizational politics, people issues, changes in policies and global events directly affect a business organization and its decisions on competition. These complexities overlay such matters as IT governance and radical changes in IT hardware, software and the networking environment. Hygiene factors and behavioural factors that contribute to the elements comprising agency theory also add to the possible outcomes in the permutations that can be made in this already complex environment (summarized in Figure 5.8).

To obtain data for the RDS, informal, semi-structured interviews are conducted. As opposed to the formal or structured interviews that have an explicit agenda, informal interviews have a specific but implicit research agenda. Informal interviews can be used to determine the categories of meaning in a culture and are useful in discovering what people think and how one person's perceptions of risk compare with another's. There is no standard measure of default values or tolerance levels in organizational performance. The empirical qualitative research method hence is suggested for the collection of risk data for the project. The observations can include nuances of behaviour of key stakeholders and key risk drivers following the specific observations.

Data on risks and risk exposure

Primary data can be gathered using planned and structured interviews, focus group sessions and the Delphi technique. This technique was developed by the Rand Corporation in the late 1960s as a forecasting methodology. Later, the US Government enhanced it as a group decision-making tool using the results of Project HINDSIGHT, which established a factual basis for the workability of Delphi. Planned and semi-structured personal interviews were conducted with current personnel from various departments as well as business consultants in the team. The interviews were designed to assess the interviewees' responses to the risks involved in the outsourcing exercise. The information gathered was then used to construct questionnaires, develop the risk dimensions and subsequently measure some of the risk exposure values. In the focus group sessions for example, the personnel from the IT planning area gathered specific information on risks in the area of IT planning. The Delphi technique was subsequently used to 'guide' debate through the discussion sessions in order to obtain the relevant information on the risks and risks dimensions required.

The research involved data accumulated through the author's work with multiple organizations on ITO projects. Secondary data was obtained from commercial project documentation as well as commonly available sources such as project reports, the Internet and other available data on the IT function within the organization. Certain key assumptions and concepts provide the basis for the exercise. The first is the concept of causality and random activity used when observing the risks that occur during the ITO exercise, as previously discussed. The other idea used is that of external influences on activities in the same exercise.

Interaction between categories

Inherent in the operations of the organization are technical, financial and operational risk. An interpretation of the types of risks that are categorized in each of these areas is subjective. This can change as the exercise changes. It is most relevant and critical, however, that use of the tool and its concept is observed and applied throughout the ITO exercise.

The tool that is proposed has been used to identify previously neglected areas of risk that the buyer organization may carry. For example, the business risks that increase as a result of the outsourcing exercise include the responsibility for the results delivered by the supplier organization. Should the supplier not deliver as promised, it is the buyer organization that ultimately suffers. The increased risk that the buyer organization carries needs to be mitigated. Before this step, however, it must identify where its tolerance for risk along the business risk dimension lies.

In many instances, as outsourcing is an accepted way of getting superior results, the specialist services offered by the supplier must be 'better' than those of the buyer. Often the ability to focus (core competency), economies of scale and financial support are advantages that the supplier has in its arsenal to assist in providing these services. Many ITO agreements fail, however, when there are disagreements on the use of these resources as both buyer and supplier require unfettered access. The RDS also provides a scenario where the benefits and risks can be illustrated and thus fairly shared. This means that the patterns or signatures are modified to the extent that both organizations benefit.

It is proposed that the RDS exercise is not one that should be conducted procedurally without an understanding of the exercise through observation, involvement and application of artistic management. It has been demonstrated that the complexities and variables involved are far too intricate for a mathematical model to be derived. This does not in any way contradict the use of the methodology for the construction of the RDS described previously. It is the combined use of heuristics, current observations and qualitative findings that plays a vital role in achieving an accurate and usable result.

Section III

Mitigating (& managing)
risks in IT outsourcing

6 Risk characteristics and behaviour in an ITO exercise

There is a need to control the characteristics and behaviour of risks to reduce the effects of those risks. Risk mitigation activity is an essential component part of the process of ensuring predictable outcomes for the ITO exercise, and consequently also of being able to derive maximum benefits from the ITO exercise itself. Risk mitigation tasks are part of good project management. It is more effective, however, if project managers have the ability to translate information on possible risks into useful knowledge. With this knowledge, both the buyer and the supplier organizations can formulate a set of practical responses to reduce the effects of risk. Targeted communications programmes, actions and policies can then be put into place using this information, to reduce the effects of risks. This will, in turn, increase confidence levels and allow ITO to be more readily accepted.

In an ITO exercise, the RDS tool introduced earlier allows risks to be identified and illustrated in order to make it possible to control them. The information gathered is used to examine risk behaviour and the various forms of risk profiles formed. Additional steps can then be taken to reduce the anticipated harmful effects of risks on the range of departments in and functions of an organization.

It is, however, often impracticable to measure events or risks that have not yet even taken place. In addition, there are many risks that are not yet defined but may, nevertheless, occur. As demonstrated in the previous chapters, the RDS tool allows the selected risk elements, together with causes and influencing factors, to be differentiated for management attention and subsequent control. This again is occasionally insufficient to represent all the risks dimensions, which may change over time. Change makes the one-time portrait or snapshot of risks constructed with the RDS quickly obsolete. In order, therefore, to anticipate risk patterns over time, the interaction between risk dimensions and the behaviour of risks in an ITO exercise needs to be observed and mapped to identify specific patterns or trends, as will be illustrated in this chapter.

The old adage 'to expect the unexpected' can be invaluable advice in a situation like IT outsourcing (ITO). Frequently, the occurrence of unexpected events directly influences other events, which eventually thwarts the objectives of the outsourcing process. It is challenging to monitor all facets of risk without using an instrument like the RDS. Many cases of ITO failures have been reported and, as a consequence, outsourcing projects are quickly seen to be of dubious worth or, even worse, deemed to be unworthy of consideration; therefore, in the latter scenario, managers prefer to avoid this topic altogether. This means that outsourcing projects and, therefore, also the business benefits thereof, are never taken advantage of.

With the RDS tool, risks are measured and translated in a meaningful format for the people who manage the projects and drive the organization's activities to work with. Having measured and understood (see the MUM methodology in Figure 6.1) the risks that become manifest in the ITO project, managers will then need to formulate a specific action agenda to mitigate these risks using the RDS instrument. Figure 6.1 is repeated below from Chapter 2.

This chapter introduces new ideas, possibly abstract in nature but important in the process whereby risks can be mitigated. Techniques based on research and practical experience gained from multiple ITO projects are introduced as the ideas are presented. A peculiar phenomenon described in this chapter appears

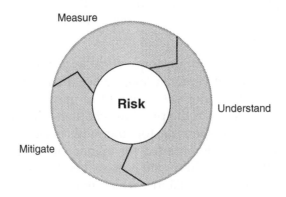

Figure 6.1
Managing risks in an IT outsourcing environment (Tho, 2003)

to consistently portray the behaviour of risks in the ITO environment. This observation is then used to predict some of the changes and behaviour of risks that manifest themselves in the ITO scenario. A significant part of this chapter is devoted to concepts and ideas, because this is an area that bridges the gap between the understanding of risks and actually mitigating them.

Risks behave by nature unpredictably but, if a structured and methodical analytical process is followed, it has been discovered that certain patterns can be identified that allow predictability, albeit with selected constraints. It is very important to *intelligently apply* the concepts introduced here and not to use them 'as-is'. To assist in this process, I have also included a case study in Chapter 8 that shows some of the concepts being applied. The slight modification of what is described in this chapter illustrates and reinforces the point that the framework proposed acts only as a guide and must be customized to the reader's own requirements.

6.1 Behaviour of risks

As with the definition of outsourcing given in Chapter 1, it is often taken as a benefit that operational risks are mitigated by the buyer organization 'passing' them to the supplier of ITO services. As such, operational risks are 'passed' from the buyer to the supplier organization when the IT function is outsourced (Bensaou, 1999). When the operational risks are transferred out, however, the risks along the legal, financial and strategic risk dimensions are observed to increase (see also examples in Chapter 8).

Although the other risks that exist are totally unrelated to operational risks, the risk dimensions that relate to them appear to change as if to compensate for the loss in operational risks. These changes occur to the extent that the total risk exposure for the particular ITO exercise remains relatively constant. This apparent interrelationship is always observed (see also further observations in Chapter 7). The various assumptions and suppositions that have been made are outlined in this chapter and in Chapter 7.

Many of the estimates of the probability of an occurrence, and also the possibility or prospect of loss, are based on heuristics or previous experience. To qualify an observation made, we need a comprehensive set of data. The structured approach suggested in Section II provides a framework in which risks can be identified. This does not mean, however, that *all* possible risks can be identified. Some risks that will not have been included would account for a shortfall or access risk exposure for the organization. It was also proposed in the previous chapter that if the relationship between cause and effect could be determined, then not all the risks would have to be defined at the outset.

Another important observation is that a specific relationship exists between several risk dimensions in an ITO exercise at any point in time. This implies the presence of linkages or a correlation between these risk dimensions. The complex causal models introduced in the previous section and illustrated via one-to-many and many-to-one relationships also contribute to a supposition that the risk dimensions exhibit some form of risk relationship pattern. Observations made from a variety of perspectives provide evidence to show the presence of definitive links between the risk dimensions in a relationship of this type.

Risks do not react or move on command. Instead, risks generally appear to change according to various causes and extraneous factors. Although the causal framework has the connotation of determinism and necessity, in practice causal relations are much more subtle and less straightforward than they may initially appear. An example of a causal relationship is the scenario where drinking alcohol and/or talking on a mobile phone while driving causes accidents. This does not actually mean that the consequences are likely or certain. By way of analogy, it is more accurate to say that the probability of an accident increases when driving under the influence of alcohol or driving while having a conversation on a mobile phone. The accident risk exposure however, has increased in these circumstances.

Failure to make IT system backups, to look at another example, does not imply an inability to recover from a hard-disk failure. The practical notion of causation requires the ability to express it in various degrees of likelihood or probability. In the instance of ITO, the causality assumption can also be observed through the myriad factors that influence the ITO exercise. This is made more complex over time as the combination of events and activities also change. The effects of events and actions are related to observable causes. Multiple causes, however, also overlay one another at different points along a timeline and blur the ability to observe a direct relationship in this phenomenon. It is important that causality is embedded and mixed within the original concepts of creation and random occurrence. In comparison with the development of models explaining the effects of empirical observations, there has been relatively little development of formal models to account for the effects of such prior knowledge.

6.2 Risk appetite

Imagine an individual managing an IT operation for an organization wishing for the mythical 'perfect project', i.e. the project or business venture that carries no risks. In this fabricated scenario, all activities proceed as planned. The organization in this instance has no risk appetite and cannot tolerate any risks at all. It is a situation where there is either a zero probability of any undesirable outcome, or a situation where the loss incurred as a result of an undesirable outcome is always zero.

A more reasonable and realistic view of things, however, is a scenario where the project is barraged with outcomes that are both undesirable and unsolicited. We also find that most organizations have a certain level of tolerance for things that may go wrong, i.e. a level or appetite for risks; the risk exposure values are actively managed within 'acceptable' or tolerable levels. These tolerable levels of risk are referred to as the 'appetite for risk' of the organization (see also 'risk appetite' in Chapter 5).

An organization's appetite for risk is distinctive as it is largely dependent on selected characteristics of the organization. For example (largely exaggerated to convey the point), a diversified conglomerate that is heavily funded may have a relatively higher tolerance for financial risk (or a larger appetite for risk) compared to a small organization that is owned by an individual, with a relatively lower appetite for financial risks. The smaller organization would not have the capability to recover from a financial disaster as well as the larger organization with significantly greater monetary reserves that it can call upon.

6.3 Fundamental assumptions in understanding risks

Three fundamental assumptions have been made so far, which are outlined below.

Cause & effect

The first is that all risks are subject to a cause and effect relationship. The causes, however, manifest themselves as either naturally occurring or through direct intervention (i.e. through careful planning and deliberate action). The observable interaction between internal and external influences on the risk exposure features cause and effect. This shows the existence of a direct relationship between the risk dimensions. For example, we say 'A caused B'. We know A occurred and B occurred, and if A had not occurred then neither would B. Bayesian theory would determine the probability of the occurrence. In this instance, however, extending these notions on categorization, we assume that the effects of the risks categorized in risk dimensions are pooled and already considered when observing the empirical data. Simply put, the risk dimensions hence have already pooled the effects of the risks. This assumes that the risks in the same common pool have common causes.

Internal/external influences

In the second assumption, the internal-influences phenomenon is limited to an individual organization as opposed to a group of interacting organizations. For example, where the RDSs for two suppliers competing for the same project are illustrated, the interaction between internal influences is only for the individual suppliers (or intra-organizational). The same logic is extended to assume the alternative situation; that is, there is a relationship between external influences only in an inter-organizational situation. This assumption is different from the other two as it breaks down quickly in practice. The classification of influences as 'internal' and 'external' does not apply; the influences combine in effects on risks. This assumption is deliberately maintained, however, to show the distinction between the competing environment (external influences) and organizational strategy (internally controlled).

Accuracy of risk classification/grouping

The third major assumption is that the risk classifications reflect the risks in the ITO exercise sufficiently to provide an accurate illustration of the risk landscape. Risks experienced in an ITO exercise are categorized into the eight dimensions crafted, discussed, tested and verified against several scenarios in the previous chapters. While these dimensions apply to the majority of ITO exercises, in others and for some types of organization, this may not be the case as risks are subject to and have a relationship with the prevailing conditions (as discussed in Chapter 3).

6.4 Effects of influences

Suppose all the risks experienced are caused by events and actions, whether purposeful or otherwise. These events and actions become influences, originating from either internal or external sources. It is intuitive then to assume that the risks experienced in an ITO exercise are related to changes in the environment, practices in the market and internal operations. Since the risk dimensions proposed correlate to the influences, the risk dimensions themselves may be used as indicators for the factors influencing the risks. To investigate the difference in external influences, the RDS profile for one organization is taken over two separate points in time (see case study in Chapter 8). Differences would be expected to originate predominantly from external influences.

It is the specific nature of this relationship between risk dimensions that is observed. Clues to its behaviour are sought by observing changes in the RDS patterns. Although the risk exposure values are dynamic, it is not certain if the *total risk exposure*[1] for the project itself changes. The background and reasons for a static total risk exposure cannot be expounded in this book but, supposing there is an observed state of stasis over time, then the dynamics of the changes in risk exposure can be managed more effectively.

6.5 Relationships between risk dimensions

Many propositions have been raised that cover the relationships between the supplier and buyer organization in an ITO exercise including agency theory and possibilities of some sharing of risks between the participating organizations. While there are relationships between the risk dimensions observed within an organization (i.e. either buyer or supplier), there are also relationships between risk dimensions between organizations (i.e. both the buyer and supplier).

The changes in the risk dimensions also appear to be *time-related* functions. That is to say, the dynamics of change along all the dimensions change with time. At any single point in time, all the risk dimensions in the RDS profile are constant. The *magnitude* of risk exposure (RE) along any of the risk dimensions changes. The changes hence are also functions of magnitude. The degree of *interrelatedness* between each risk dimension also appears to change, giving rise to a third function. The changes are a function of degree of relatedness. A brief discussion on notion of risk balancing later in this chapter provides further background.

---

[1] Previously defined as the mathematical sum of risk exposure along all the risk dimensions in an IT outsourcing exercise

Further, there are three key characteristics that are exhibited by the risks in this situation. These characteristics include the risk balancing phenomenon, the concept of total risk exposure and the existence of a state of equilibrium.

Risk balancing

In an ITO environment, risk profiles are often short-lived, i.e. they change rapidly in response to changes in the environment. Peculiar to outsourcing, there are two very closely linked organizations: the buyer and the supplier. Both these organizations work towards a 'win–win' situation where the risks are almost equally shared. This state of 'risk balance' provides the most equitable form of partnership where both parties are motivated to jointly reduce the risk exposure. In a 'risk balanced' state, the risk areas (bounded by the risk signature) for the buyer and supplier are almost the same, and a state of equilibrium is reached where both participants share almost equal risks.

Changes in risk exposure (RE)

As previously proposed, the risk exposure depicted by the RDS is demonstrated by the equation simplified in Chapter 4 and re-illustrated below for reference.

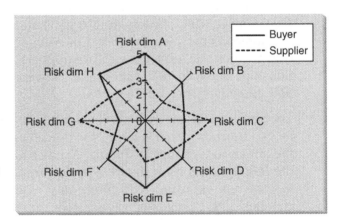

Figure 6.2
Re-illustration of the RDS equation (from Figure 4.2 in Chapter 4)

$$\sum \text{Risk} = 0.5\sin\theta \left[\sum_{i=1}^{i=7} (\text{risk}_i \times \text{risk}_{(i+1)}) + (\text{risk}_1 \times \text{risk}_8) \right]$$

But $\theta = 45°$ where there are 8 dimensions. Therefore,

$$\sum \text{Risk} = \alpha \left[\sum_{i=1}^{i=7} (\text{risk}_i \times \text{risk}_{(i+1)}) + (\text{risk}_1 \times \text{risk}_8) \right]$$

where $\alpha = 0.3536$

The equation carries a constant α, that is dependent on the number of risk dimensions in the ITO exercise. The value of α is calculated. The total risk exposure changes are the total risk profile changes. When the number of risk dimensions change, then the value of α also changes, where $\alpha = \sin(360/(\# \text{ risk dimensions}))$. Sample values of α are listed in Table 4.1 in Chapter 4.

Through simplification the *total risk exposure*, Λ, or area under the RDS with a selected profile, can be easily computed as $\Lambda = \alpha$ (Σ (product of adjacent risk magnitudes)), where α is a constant depending on the number of risk dimensions. Then, assuming $\{\alpha \ [\Sigma \ (\text{product of adjacent risk magnitudes})]\}$ is a constant at one point in time we can represent this signature as a constant, beta (β). These changes are therefore observed to be almost zero over time for any particular ITO exercise. This is also demonstrated in the case study exercise in Chapter 8, and is observed to apply to the buyer organization and its total risk exposure profile over time.

State of equilibrium

When both the buyer and supplier are considered together and assuming a natural state where $\delta\Lambda$ (buyer) $\neq \delta\Lambda$ (supplier), then the objective is to achieve a situation of equilibrium where the risks are described mathematically as

$$\int_0^\infty \beta(\text{buyer}).dt - \int_0^\infty \beta(\text{supplier}).dt = 0$$

over time, for both the supplier and buyer organizations. Any fluctuations in risk exposure for $\delta\Lambda$ (buyer) should, through negotiations, control and governance, be also reflected for $\delta\Lambda$ (supplier). The use of the infinite limit is for illustrative purposes only, i.e. to show that over time the buyer and supplier would reach agreements that determine equity for both sides.

In summary, the equation describes a situation over a significant amount of time, when the buyer and the supplier profiles would be the same. In an RDS, there are an infinite number of variables that need to be accounted for; also risks are not forces of nature but a humanly derived concept. The concept of a state of equilibrium also exists when the RDS is perfectly octagonal (for eight risk dimensions). This is the state where the risk exposure in all the dimensions is the same and there is no further need to trade one risk off against another. The magnitude of the risk exposure, i.e. the area bounded by the octagonal RDS profile, then needs to be reduced.

By way of comparison, the analogy of the lever, where the magnitude of the force and distance away from the fulcrum can be controlled, can be applied to both the risk exposure (β) signature, and time (t), through an understanding of the relationships between risk dimensions. The fact that the two equations involved simplify to two controllable variables is completely coincidental. The main assumption, however, is that the variables can be controlled via the manipulation of events, actions or activities.

The RDS profiles in this chapter can be extended to show the risk balancing phenomenon which was observed during the exercise. Risk balancing occurs when several events are made to occur in order to mitigate the risks along one of the risk dimensions, which affects other risk dimensions to the extent that an almost perfect octagon is achieved. By way of analogy, this is much like a see-saw where there is a relationship between the load and distance from the fulcrum where Work (W) = Load (L) × Distance (D) from the fulcrum (Figure 6.3). This is a simplistic example where the see-saw will come to rest in a horizontal state when W^1 and W^2 are equal.

The analogy ends where there are a finite number of variables in the equation for the lever; moreover the lever is governed by the laws of motion. This is, however, consistent with the observations made during this exercise. Each time the risk factors and risk exposure are high (indicated by a spike in the RDS), the risks from another risk dimension can be used to reduce the first dimension. The case study (see Chapter 8) describes a suitable environment to observe this phenomenon. It has been shown

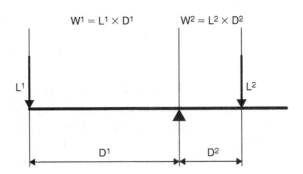

Figure 6.3

The lever and forces in equilibrium

that there is a direct and immediate relationship between the risk dimensions to the extent that the risk exposures along each of them compensate for the increase or reduction in the others until the total risk exposure for the organization's ITO exercise reverts to the original value.

There is a period over which the total risk exposure appears constant. There is also a period, which could be many times longer, when the total risk exposure for both the supplier and the buyer is the same. Two major areas where the new understanding of these characteristics of risk dimensions could be helpful include the determination of strategies to shape the risk profile to within an organization's tolerance limits, and the optimal duration of ITO contracts.

6.6 Game theory

Game theory is another perspective that can be used to describe conditions in which different types of organizational arrangements develop and change. It involves the interaction between individuals or organizations. McMillan (1992) mentions that game theory 'is a study of rational behaviour in situations involving interdependence'. The notion of equilibrium and a state of constancy observed in the scenarios in this chapter are arguably closely coupled with game theory.

Game theory is not concerned with defining objectives, designing the alternatives or assessing the consequences where these are considered as being of external derivation or previously determined from the RDS data. It offers two main approaches. The first exploits criteria of choice developed in a broader context by game theory, as for example the max–min rule, where we choose the alternative such that the worst possible consequence of the chosen alternative is better than (or equal to) the best possible consequence of any other alternative. The second approach is to reduce the uncertainty in the case of risk by using subjective probabilities, based on expert assessments or on analysis of previous decisions made in similar circumstances. With information from the RDS and relationships between each risk dimension, the alternative actions by the team will have one of several possible consequences. The probability of occurrence for each consequence can be computed and hence each alternative can be associated with a probability distribution. The decision-makers hence can make choices among probability distributions. When the probability distributions are unknown, one speaks about decision under uncertainty. Game theory then ranks the possible decisions using a set of criteria consistent with the decision-maker's objectives and preferences.

The payoffs for the variety of situations that occur between the buyer and supplier also represent various conflicts. In this situation, gains and losses may be unequally distributed, which allows the representation of numerous competitive and conflict situations. Game theory then proposes several solutions, e.g. in a min–max strategy each of the participants minimizes the maximum loss the other can impose on him; a mixed strategy involves probabilistic choices. Experiments with such games revealed conditions for co-operation, defection and the persistence of conflict. If we combine this scenario with the theory postulated earlier, i.e. that the total risk exposure is in a state of constancy throughout the exercise where the dynamics of the risks along each risk dimension compensate for one another in the course of the exercise, then there is a state where there is an equilibrium to be reached. There is no overriding winning strategy that either the buyer or the supplier needs to make.

When the observations and theories proposed in the previous sections are compared with the component parts of game theory, then the connection is not as far fetched as it may initially appear. It lies very much in the interaction between the supplier and the buyer organizations which, in turn, determine and influence the risk profiles. This was used in the context of formulating a tool for the understanding of information services outsourcing (Elitzur and Wensley, 1997). A situation in game theory arises where the Nash equilibrium is observed (Nash, 1951; 1953). A Nash equilibrium situation arises where a set of strategies of all players in a game exists when no player has incentive to deviate from his strategy given that the other players do not deviate. The mathematical principles of game theory involve an analysis of interactions among various economic players. This is highlighted here for comparative purposes in relation to the ITO exercise.

The point needs to be raised that a situation might develop in which the total risk exposure remains constant despite the changes in the risk profile. This supports the argument where the strategies of both the supplier and the buyer also reach equilibrium with knowledge of this state. This concept can be explored further to include the ability and interaction of the parties – buyer and supplier – to influence the RDS. In his paper, Nash focused on rivalries in which all players could benefit, showing that there were solutions to game theory problems in which no player would be able to do better than any other player, even if one player knew what the other players were doing. Nash distinguished between co-operative games, in which binding agreements are made, and non co-operative games, in which binding agreements are not feasible. The Nash equilibrium appears appropriate in the context of this discussion as it provides further explanation for equilibrium in the risk profiles. This situation also involves two (or more) players over a period of time, and in constant negotiation with each other, allowing the application of Nash's theory.

In order to take this argument further, extensive experimental evidence and data will need to be collected from both buyer and supplier organizations. In this context, however, it is noted that the experiment would need to cover all the parameters mentioned in the earlier chapters including the factors influencing the creation of the RDS in the first place. In combination, many of the simplistic and theoretical examples made in this section would provide the complete picture that is theorized, to follow the equilibria proposed by Nash. This would have to be the subject for another book.

6.7 Chaos theory

If the risk profiles are taken and viewed from yet another perspective, that is, as chaotic systems (Baker and Gollub, 1990) and using chaos theory (Lorenz, 1993), the initial observations, curiously, are also substantiated. It is known that even the smallest imaginable discrepancy between two sets of initial conditions would always result in a huge discrepancy at later or earlier times in any system following chaos theory. Here, chaotic systems are mathematically deterministic, that is, they follow precise laws. The irregular behaviour of chaotic systems appears to the casual observer to be random. The presence of chaotic systems in nature also appears to place a limit on our ability to apply deterministic physical laws to predict risks with any degree of certainty. The discovery of chaos therefore implies that randomness lurks at the core of any deterministic model such as the one discussed in this book. The complexity and uncertainty of the risk influences notion made earlier were designed to argue the fact that a conclusive link may never be found.

Amid the apparent confusion, however, patterns of natural equilibrium were observed. There were clues that become evidence in support of a form of constancy in the total risk exposure in the patterns in the RDS illustrations. The observed equilibrium over time supports the observations of constancy in the data that were examined. If there is a state of equilibrium, then the idea of a relationship between the risks dimensions that compensates for changes between them is also supported. This, in turn, supports the thinking and general notion that a clear relationship exists between risk dimensions in an ITO exercise that allows the total risk exposure levels to reach a state of equilibrium over time.

The arguments for development of the notion that risk relationships exist are strengthened as observations are made from alternative perspectives. There is no defeat in admitting to chaos; rather, facing the problem provides the practitioner with a management challenge that is integral to managing in this environment. Outsourcing arrangements in their simplest forms involve two organizations, the buyer and supplier. The models that were introduced included agency theory and game theory, which have already been used to describe many of the situations in which the ITO arrangement operates. The association with game theory (between the buyer and supplier organizations) and semblances of the Nash equilibrium does not completely justify this but supports the observations of an equilibrium in the risk profiles occurring in the ITO exercise. Authors Elitzur and Wensley (1997) followed a similar path and placed emphasis on the observable phenomenon of risk sharing in an ITO exercise. They also attempted to provide game theory interpretations of key aspects of ITO arrangements. This study provides an alternative and comprehensive view of this theory through specific models that have been constructed in the ITO arrangement.

6.8 The perfect project

There has never been an attempt to describe the illusory 'perfect project' described at the start of the chapter, nor any endeavour to predict risks. The observations described in this chapter were designed to build additional rigour into the risk assessment framework, which is constantly being reconstructed and refined. The manager's idealistic dreams mentioned earlier may never be realized but the observations from the RDS support the proposition that the relationship between the selected risk dimensions that arise in the outsourcing of the IT function results in a constant total risk exposure for both the supplier and buyer organizations.

There appears to be no set of 'rules' that govern the interrelationship. The interrelationships between each of these events and the risk exposure can be described as being 'complementarily interconnected', i.e. they affect each other. There is no direct cause-and-effect relationship that can be observed. The essential characteristics of the interaction cannot be neglected either as some features can be used to mitigate some effects of risk. Although rules provide some structure for the analysis, they also divert attention from key observations; i.e. risks are outcomes or a set of events that by their very nature cannot be predetermined accurately. The concept of risk balancing involves the proposition that risk exposure tends to settle into a state of equilibrium after a period of time. This supports the notion that all risks in all dimensions are interrelated.

Over a period of time relationships are observed to reach a state of equilibrium. A natural state of equilibrium for total risk exposure is proposed. In this natural state, the total risk exposure for an organization (either the buyer or the supplier) remains constant over time. This is also the state in which the fluctuations in risk exposure for the buyer are mirrored for the supplier. In the midst of all the activities, events and changes in the environment, the total risk exposure for the buyer equals that for the supplier. The apparent harmonious relationship between the organizations is reached where both organizations have a mutually beneficial and synergistic existence. Examples of this are observed in many outsourcing relationships that have survived over significant periods of time. If these observations are true, this is expected for ITO relationships (which are relatively recent) moving forwards.

After the rigour of developing models and defining risk categories, conclusions were reached using a set of heuristics and trends from observations of risk exposure and outcomes within the boundaries of an ITO exercise, also incorporating both internal and external features of the business landscape influencing the interaction between the actions and subsequent events. The next chapter describes this risk relationship notion further and concludes the study with some final observations before the case study is introduced to show the application of these concepts in the management of risks in this environment.

7

Mitigating risks in an ITO environment

Mitigate: origins lie in the Latin mitigare, *to make mild;*
mitis, *gentle or soft; and* agere; *to do.*
15th century vocabulary

An enduring task of a manager in a typical ITO exercise is to reduce risks. There is no discrimination regarding the type of risks that will need attention, and risks along any of the dimensions where risk exposure has obviously exceeded the organization's appetite for risk may need to be mitigated. A manager might also proactively forecast risks that may eventually exceed the organization's risk tolerance limits. The task is never-ending because risks are dynamic and risk influences are always present.

As risks are transferred to the supplier benefit derived by the buyer organization arises through reduction in risk exposure along, for example, the operational and technical risk dimensions, for which the supplier is compensated with a fee. In addition, the supplier's financial and business risks relating to the ITO exercise are observed to decrease. This shift in risk exposure values is a phenomenon that is fairly predictable.

Risks along each of the dimensions demonstrate distinctive patterns of behaviour. For example, in the previous chapter, it was shown that a relationship exists between risk dimensions to the extent that, in one instance, the total risk exposure for a project remained constant over time. This was repeatedly observed in the same ITO exercise, and the same phenomenon is seen over many different projects. As illustrated in Section II, the RDS tool allows risk exposure to be mapped on the various risk dimensions. The method for mitigating the risks described here, utilizes this unique behaviour.

7.1 The ITO risk ecosystem

The state of equilibrium mentioned earlier is where the *total risk exposure* is constant. This applies when variables like the type of organization, time and selected ITO exercise remain constant.

These variables are found in what is described as an ITO 'risk ecosystem'. The risk ecosystem borrows the term 'ecosystem', which was coined in 1935 by the British ecologist Sir Arthur George Tansley, who described the living and nonliving parts of natural systems as being in 'constant interchange'. In this ecosystem, the sum total of risks is constant as the risk dimensions are in a constant state of flux and interchange. The correspondence with the ITO scenario allows the RDS tool to be used and fairly accurate predictions to be made based on the notion that specific relationships exist between the risk dimensions in the outsourcing of the IT function. The relationship between the risk dimensions allows changes to take place along each risk dimension to the extent that the mathematical sum total of all the risk exposure elements remains *constant*. The state of equilibrium exists to the extent that a *natural* state of equilibrium exists, previously described mathematically and restated here as:

$$\int_0^\infty \beta(buyer).dt - \int_0^\infty \beta(supplier).dt = \text{constant}$$

where β represents the total risk exposure.

Risks are, to a reasonable extent, naturally occurring. The risk ecosystem is a balance between forces. The analogy of nature's ecosystem illustrates this point. A popular predator–prey model is a concept where, initially, there are a given number of predators that feed on a given number of prey. As the number of prey reduce because of hunting activity, the scarcity of food (prey) forces a reduction in the number of predators. Fewer predators means that more prey have a chance to survive as the prey is then not hunted. The numbers of prey subsequently increase. The cycle then repeats. As the number of prey increases, so does the number of predators. The predator/prey ecosystem sustains a relatively stable number of prey and predators at any given point in time. The concept of the risk ecosystem appears to exhibit similar, although not identical, behaviour. Both the supplier and buyer risk profiles appear to fluctuate as the risk is passed from one organization to the other. Over time, there appears to be a stable total risk profile for both buyer and supplier.

The notion of equilibrium and a state of constancy was compared earlier with game theory in a situation where the buyer and supplier organizations were exposed to a series of decisions over the life cycle of the ITO exercise. This was previously proposed by Elitzur and Wensley (1997). In this case, however, the emphasis was on a state of equilibrium in the total risk exposure experienced by the buyer and supplier organizations. New insight into this case is gained through observing a state of equilibrium that exists as the influences or causes of risks are considered. The result was equilibrium in the totality of the state of risk exposure.

7.2 Predicting the behaviour of risks with the RDS

The behaviour of risks in an ITO exercise, using the RDS, can therefore be summarized as follows. In an ITO exercise, risks are transferred from one organization to another over the period agreed under an earlier defined contract. The total risk exposure of the contracting parties remains relatively constant within the selected risk ecosystem. Within the risk ecosystem that has been defined, the constancy of the total risk exposure patterns does not appear to be affected by either internal or external risk influences. This special relationship between risk dimensions appears to remain and is only affected by the functions of time, magnitude of risk types and the degree of interrelatedness of risk dimensions.

The function of time is a dominant feature as the effects of risk occur over varying lengths of time. For each risk effect to completely express itself, the variable of time needs to be taken into account as much as the variability of the effect of the risk itself. If a risk type is known to take effect over a longer period, and the time variable can be controlled, then the risk may be mitigated using this variable.

The magnitude of risk is a component of the risk exposure defined earlier, and a high risk exposure carries along with it a high risk magnitude. If the impact of risks along a dimension is of high magnitude, this often overrides concerns for risks with relatively lower magnitude. For a given organizational risk appetite, risks with low magnitudes may sometimes also be considered immaterial and ignored. Hence the risk relationship equation can be put into effect to mitigate risks. For example, mitigation of a risk of low magnitude may be ignored altogether given an organization with high risk appetite for this type of risk.

Often also, risks of different types and from different dimensions relate to each other closely. For example, the risk dimensions for strategy, business and environment are very frequently grouped together because of the very close relationship they enjoy.

All three affect each other very closely. Other cases, operations for example, may not be affected at all by the environment.

There are many major factors that have a role in the interaction between the selected risk dimensions. Attention has been drawn here to the three salient variables which emerge as more significant than the others.

7.3 Depiction of the risk profile

Despite steps taken to verify all the elements that contribute to the risk profiles, it is arguable how well the description or postulation of the behaviour of the interaction between the risks in the various risk dimensions identified can be used in other ITO projects. A major assumption made is that the profiles provide a sufficiently accurate illustration of the profiles that are observed. The consistency of methods in the process, standardized measurement techniques and common tools negate possible errors in measurement. While the risk patterns and observed interaction between the risk dimensions are verified against theoretical models, many of the pragmatic answers come from experience and heuristics. The use of theoretical models is useful to the extent that they predict certain types of behaviour and become powerful tools when used in conjunction with experience and a little common sense.

The RDS, simply used, can already provide a graphical illustration that highlights these risk dimensions that require urgent and immediate reaction. For a more proactive stance, the RDS can also provide a framework for risk mitigation through the recognition of risk patterns that arise from the interaction between supplier and buyer. Strategic interaction can be validated with game theory. The behaviour of people and interaction derives from agency theory. The risk variation and behaviour of relationships between the risks can be related to Nash's theory. The extent of risk exposure can then often be predicted via the theory that the total risk exposure remains constant over time in a risk ecosystem (Tho, 2004). In combination this allows the manager to forecast, to a limited degree, the behaviour of risks in the ITO space.

7.4 Risk frameworks

There are critiques that may be made of the existing techniques and frameworks. First, the models are limited in the ability to capture and illustrate all the risks that occur. Then again, the models are focused on specific risks, which leads to arguments about accuracy and determination in an environment where uncertainty and a high degree of change are prevalent. Finally, the assumptions made using the existing models possibly do not allow for the specialized need for observations in the transferability of risks across organizations. While these points are true to a limited extent, there are also those that need to be raised in defence of the use of these frameworks that highlight the significant advantages that outweigh these points.

In order to observe the interaction of the group of identified risks, an alternative perspective is recommended. Instead of viewing risks within an organization, an outside or macro-view of the total risk profile (all of the risks combined) can be taken. The difference is that both the environmental and internal risks can be viewed together. This addresses some of the shortcomings of the earlier framework in the ability to capture all the risks. The method of grouping risks into categories (which refer to both internal and external risks) allows a summary illustration of the majority of risks that are perceived to become manifest in one illustration.

Many of the rules and frameworks used originate from existing risk frameworks. As the risks are studied from a complete risk profile perspective, the nuances of each risk item are considered as part of the collective for the risk group or risk dimension. This reduces the complexity of the study and allows a clearer view of the phenomenon where risks appear to be 'transferred' from one organization to another in an ITO agreement.

From the new perspective, risks are viewed as a whole where all the risks that affect the ITO project are taken. Following detailed observation of the new risk profile, the total risk profile of the ITO project remains constant over time. Information that supports this argument includes observations of empirical data from the RDS that show changes in the individual risk dimensions. The profiles from observations of the RDS profile show that changes occur along risk dimensions, appearing to compensate for changes along other risk dimensions that have arisen earlier.

The shifts in magnitude of total risk exposure value from the buyer to the supplier in the operational and technical risks dimensions are 'compensated for' by movements in the risks along other dimensions for both organizations. As the supplier accepts the transfer of risk in the operation and technical dimensions (i.e. increases along these risk dimensions), the supplier organization is also observed to experience less risk exposure from the business, strategic and financial risk perspectives. Both buyer and supplier organizations experience many changes along the individual risk dimensions but the total risk profile remains constant. The supplier is able to enter into a long-term agreement with the buyer because its risk profile is fairly uniform.

Interplay between risk dimensions

Assuming that the eight dimensions mentioned earlier accurately depicted the different risks that become manifest in the ITO, the interplay between the risk dimensions was investigated. In order to limit the number of assumptions that could be made, the investigation was peculiar only to the outsourcing of the IT function.

In addition, the significance of IT was explained as it was unique and displayed characteristics different from those of other support or strategic functions in a typical organization. For example, given the extremely dynamic nature of the IT function, the interplay between the risk dimensions may have been affected. The ability to continually observe the total risk profile may have been influenced by the nature of the IT function in an outsourcing environment.

Interaction of intrusive factors

The interaction that exists as a result of intrusive factors (exogenous and endogenous) was assumed to play a role in the interrelationship between the risk dimensions. The risk dimensions proposed in this study provide an empirical framework to illustrate the interaction of the elements and the nature of the interaction within the risk frameworks proposed by other researchers. The evidence supports the proposition that relationships exist between these risk dimensions. The interaction of the intrusive factors assumes that the majority of the factors have been included.

7.5 Using the concepts

General theories that attempt to explain the implicit relationships that exist provide a framework, based on which further tests can be made. The methodology used in this book already enables detailed observation of the influences and risk elements for one ITO exercise. The work already completed also allows for subsequent research to be done to confirm or build upon the observations made in this study. To facilitate its use in another environment, the theories on risk relationships and interaction between risk dimensions in an ITO exercise have been formulated in this chapter.

Overcoming difficulties that may be encountered

Possible difficulties may be encountered in selected areas when attempting to work through the risk frameworks. One such area could be the issue of uncertainty in the environment and the significant variation and dynamics in the way the risk elements become manifest. The situations mentioned included a clear direction when there were high levels of certainty and discrete outcomes through a situation involving 'true ambiguity'. The situation where the ITO exercise is conducted probably lies in between, i.e. where there is a range of possible outcomes. The methods proposed are an attempt to render the quantification of risk elements a more consistent method of monitoring and managing risks. While ideas are drawn from various sources, the final derivative that is proposed is the risk dimension signature (RDS) tool. The RDS allows the focus on all risks to be managed and the focus to be shifted to critical risk elements, grouped into risk categories. As these change over the life cycle of the ITO exercise, the RDS allows the capture of the major changes in risk elements and fluctuations in risk exposure. It is not, however, a substitute for a thorough knowledge of the environment and is not a replacement for experience and judgement.

Another area of difficulty that can be encountered is project logistics and access to the appropriate sources of information (e.g. documents, people and stored data) in the organization that is in the midst of a major ITO exercise. In addition, access to the relevant information and people can prove to be extremely difficult if this is treated as a separate activity. This impediment can be reduced by appropriate initiation as an integral part of the ITO exercise itself (and executed by the ITO team). Also, given the sensitive nature of the results and the need for very senior management attention, it is recommended that there is senior management involvement and sponsorship throughout the exercise.

Yet another area of difficulty could be encountered in an ITO exercise, one that needs to be highlighted to avoid the same errors and mistakes each time this exercise is repeated: this constitutes a combination of issues starting with the logistics of the data gathering exercise, then the determination of the appropriate number and description of the risk dimensions, followed by consensus on the risk values that would be used. The sequence of events that is planned may result in the determination of the risk dimensions conducted prior to the collection of data for risk exposure along the risk dimensions. To avoid this, it should be done simultaneously to streamline logistics (i.e. time and effort). The difficulties in logistics start when some of the participants who contribute to the development of the risk dimensions are no longer on the team at the time the data are collected. The 'buy-in' and discussion time that is spent talking about the risk dimensions may prove challenging. It can be seen then that the people involved add to the subtle differences in each definition embedded in the risk dimensions. In another project, the changes were so subtle that there were up to thirty different risk dimensions at one stage. Again, based on reason and theory described at length earlier, the rational number of risk dimensions has been summarized to a manageable eight.

Limitations

A discussion on difficulty would not be complete if the limitations of the exercise were not incorporated. Limitations, in this instance, arise from the difficulties that are anticipated when using the RDS tool.

A limitation in any study of risks is the estimates made of the probabilities of losses from these risks. It would be extremely difficult, if not impossible, to accurately guess the probability of an occurrence. The number of participants is usually significant. In projects undertaken, over a hundred individuals representing approximately 10% of the organization and possibly up to three quarters of the IT division were interviewed. As a result, many of the responses provided a class 'average'. In addition, the categorization of the risk types also provided a further 'average' value. In many instances, such an exercise is not possible. Such a limitation needs to be taken into account in the results.

A further limitation of the exercise is the description of the risk exposure (RE) profile and comparison of the shapes. The area enclosed by the risk profile in the RDS represented the total risk exposure at a particular point in time. Although changes in shape can be identified through observation, more subtle changes are difficult to quantify or illustrate accurately.

There is some use of 'fuzzy logic' where the outcome of the risk elements is expressed as a probability rather than as a certainty. For example, in addition to being either true or false, the probability expressed by a participant of the exercise, to the best of their knowledge and based on heuristics, were, in relation to outcome, probably true, possibly true, possibly false, and probably false. This is a matter of heuristics because the probabilities were expressed based on experience, knowledge of the environment and the situation. In an analogous example, if a coin were to be tossed ten times and the results indicated ten occurrences of 'head', the statistical result would be '1' for head (or 100% chance of the occurrence of 'head'). We know that in an idealized example, it would be '0.5' (or 50% chance of the occurrence of 'head'). Heuristics was used in a situation where there was a decision based on judgement. In a situation where the probabilities of risks occurring were uncertain, deriving responses from the participants in the exercise involved group discussions as well as the methods discussed in the previous section.

A limitation of cognitive heuristics is the probability of error. In a situation where the probability of risk is uncertain, the bias provided by the participants based on prior and existing knowledge furnishes the platform for the data to be collected. This is also related to the first point made in this section. The assumption that has been used in all the cases discussed here was that the same errors were negated in the grouping and classification process.

Many of the limitations that have been encountered are exhibited as a result of uncertainty in the environment and in the concepts of management under uncertainty. Hamel and Prahalad (1994) have repeatedly proposed that no paradigm or idea would be useful in formulating a strategy. They mention that in an environment of uncertainty there is 'no comfort' that can be gained and that plans and strategies are indeed limited and cannot 'be reduced to eight rules for excellence, seven S's, five competitive forces, four product life cycle stages, three generic strategies, and innumerable two-by-two matrices'.

This provides a setting in which my proposition can be further analysed and extrapolated in future studies. A stand on the view of the knowledge paradigm is taken to ensure that the theories developed are 'valid'. The notion of validity or credibility of the case presented by the researcher provides a foundational element for new theory. Ultimately, however, validity depends on the collective judgement of the community that a construct and its measure are valid. In the end, we are all left to deal with the effects of our judgement, which is just as it should be.

It must be mentioned that the validity of an argument should be distinguished from the truth of the conclusion. If one or more of the premises is false, the conclusion of a valid argument that follows may also be false. With this in mind, several key assumptions have been made during the course of the arguments in this book that need to be highlighted.

Important assumptions

Several important assumptions were made in pursuing work that guided the direction of the recommendations made specifically with regard to the use of the RDS. Some of these assumptions relate to general activities and behaviour of the entities being studied and are included here for completeness. For example, it was assumed that the buyer and supplier organizations approach the exercise as rational business entities. The decisions and actions that follow are designed to enhance profitability and increase the effectiveness of the individual organizations.

It is assumed that the major theories were applicable and accurate in the context of the ITO exercise. While the exercise served to re-validate many theories, others could not be validated. For example, it was assumed that risks did not occur randomly. The theory of causality was used where there was a notion of definitive causes and effects of risks in the ITO exercise coming from both within and outwith the organization. While the causality theory could not be validated, it was assumed that it was applicable and accurate in this context.

It was further assumed that the models used to derive the experimental constants and variables for the risk profiles were sufficiently accurate. There were three sets of constant values used and two of variables. The constant figure of 8 for the risk dimensions was assumed for the project. Another constant α, (see equation (4.1), p. 98) used to compute the area under the RDS graph was based on straight lines between the risk dimensions. Finally, a constant number of supplier and buyers was assumed. Although the implications for these values carry little consequence for the final recommendation, they are highlighted to enable appropriate changes to be made the next time the exercise is run in another environment. Other values that were used included those in the six-point Likert scale, used for measurement. The other major variables that could be altered were the three major factors that appear to have influenced the relationship between the risk dimensions. The experimental constants should be reviewed each time the exercise is repeated.

The assumptions made in using the methods pertained to the area of consistency. Specifically, arguments were made on the need to group risks into categories for measurement. A key assumption arrived at was that the risk exposure measurements could be categorized. Examples from insurance and other industries were also assumed to be applicable in this context. Although the concept of categorization is accepted, there is no clear proof of the ability to compartmentalize risks and no extensive study to show that risks can be grouped.

Many of the definitions, concepts and notions were derived from the literature and were validated so far as was possible against natural laws, reason and common sense. There were three element definitions that were difficult to validate. This included a definitive meaning for the major terms used, including a universally accepted meaning for the terms outsourcing and risk exposure as well as the term organization. The researcher's definition was highlighted and clearly defined at an early stage in the book. The assumption was that the minor ambiguities in the definitions would not significantly alter the development of the main theory and ideas.

In addition, the recommendations are based on multiple case studies conducted in Asia and Australia. An assumption made is that the management style and the cultures of the individuals involved did not play a significant role in the judgement of risks, which in turn might have influenced the measurement of risks. Despite obvious documented differences in terms of Western and Asian cultures regarding 'power distance' and 'individualism', sufficient evidence was not found to differentiate the decisions made in Asia from those in Western cultures, other than the 'experience' factor. Individualism is characterized as a preference for a loosely knit social framework in societies wherein individuals are supposed to take care of themselves and their immediate families only: the 'I'-concept (Hofstede, 1980; Brislin, 1999).

Besides the major assumptions above, there were three main areas where the impact of the assumptions could have made some difference to the outcomes. These areas included the creation of the risk profile with risk dimensions, depiction of the risk profile and the construction of the theory that is discussed here.

7.6 Insights into risk behaviour using the RDS tool

Given the new insight into the behaviour of risk, measured as risk exposure values through the life cycle of the ITO exercise, the manager will have accumulated a greater appreciation of the risks involved whether directly through the RDS or indirectly through the use of the methods described.

The IT function was outsourced to derive significant benefits for the buyer organization, generally by leveraging economies of scale and the ability to focus on core competence. In most cases, the buyer is observed to pass its operational risks to the supplier and derive maximum benefit from the expertise of the supplier in terms of resources, knowledge and processes. The supplier in turn would be compensated for its participation in the exercise with a steady stream of revenue over a contracted period. The supplier then shares its resources and leverages on its own economies of scale. The question remains, however, if the supplier would carry too much risk since the operational and technical risks would be taken over from the buyer organization. The concept of the winner's curse described in Section I is a repeated phenomenon where the supplier underestimates the costs of providing the services in its zeal to capture a larger market share.

Buyers and suppliers have arrived at outsourcing agreements in many different scenarios. The outsourcing of the IT function, however, is something that has relatively recently been resorted to. It can be shown that the risk profiles of two different suppliers with different backgrounds typically are very similar. This is often because both supplier organizations operate in the same environment. In most cases, this demonstrates consistency in the perception of risk profiles by different organizations at a given point in time.

Studies that were made also demonstrate that both the buyer and supplier maintain the same total risk exposure, despite significant differences in the risk profile at different stages in the ITO exercise. Given a long-term contract (over many years), it was also theoretically demonstrated that a state of equilibrium is reached where, over time, the total risk exposure would remain constant. The buyer's risk profile is measured at several separate points in time over the life cycle of the outsourcing exercise. Most of the changes in the risk profile can then be explained through actions giving rise to environmental as well as internal influences on the project. Importantly, the total risk exposure remains fairly constant during all these events. The main theory can be expressed in the form of the fundamental equations following:

$$\int_0^\infty \beta(\text{buyer}).dt = \tau_1$$

and

$$\int_0^\infty \beta(\text{supplier}).dt = \tau_2$$

where τ_1, τ_2 are constants specific to the particular ITO exercise that is being undertaken.

7.7 Further remarks

The IT function is a 'necessary evil' that many organizations require just to stay in the market. It is a matter of survival in the current economy. Organizations use IT to enable the development and use of faster and more efficient processes and to keep the costs of production low. Some organizations use the IT function as a strategic tool that differentiates products and services from those of the competition. The majority of organizations, however, need to maintain a complex and very dynamic IT function just to support routine operations. It is these organizations that primarily are resorting to outsourcing arrangements. A new market is created where organizations seize the opportunity to supply IT services to other organizations.

For the many organizations that seek to relieve themselves of the operational risks inherent to the IT function, this study supports the notion that the operational and technical risks are indeed 'shifted' to the supplier organization. The benefit to the many organizations starting an ITO contract is the ability to shift unwanted operational and technical risks that become manifest specifically in the IT function, to the supplier.

At the same time, as the IT function changes, organizations that need to realize the strategic advantage of the IT function in differentiating services and products are also resorting to outsourcing arrangements. The strategic risks are mitigated via the use of more effective governance processes and an understanding of the total risk exposure. The results of this study also provide another perspective wherein the total risk exposure remains the same for these organizations; while some areas of risk may exceed the organization's appetite for risk, the total risk exposure is unaltered. As there are areas of high risk, there will be risk areas where the risk exposure will have reduced to compensate for the high risk effects; again, the total risk exposure is unchanged. Over time, purposeful action will shift the risks from the areas where exposure is high to the areas where exposure is low.

If the perspective of the supplier of ITO services is taken, it appears to be able to take on the new risks, although sometimes to its peril. The winner's curse phenomenon is one of several results of the neglect of the risks involved, plus an overzealous attitude by suppliers to win work and underprice their services. Again, if the concept of a relationship between the risk dimensions introduced here is used, the total risk profiles observed will reach a state of equilibrium. And, as areas of very high risk exposure appear, other areas of risk will be observed where there will be a reduction in risk exposure that compensates for the increased risk. The total risk exposure remains constant over time. Again, with management focused on mitigating risk in the areas of high exposure, the total risk profile remains unchanged. This means that in the areas of low risk exposure additional risks will be taken on in further compensation for reductions in risk in the areas of high risk exposure.

Finally, as with many other theories and propositions, the risk relationship concept in any exercise must not stand alone but be subject to 'common sense' and logical tests in environments that extend beyond the one that has been suggested here. The cases discussed here have been subject to predetermined limitations and conditions, so other tests must be used to introduce a new set of parameters.

Section II began as an attempt to explain the singular phenomenon of risk transfer that had attracted many organizations to consider the use of outsourcing to provide further benefits for the IT function. This was based very much on an organization's understanding of the nature of ITO and general concepts of risk. There are few tools or risk frameworks available to measure the risk profile of an organization in an ITO environment. The concepts of pooling risks in the insurance industry led to the notion of categorizing risks into risk dimensions. This led to the introduction of the risk dimension signature (RDS), which is unique to any individual ITO exercise; the RDS allowed observations of the risk profile to continue. The notion that there exists a relationship between changes in risk dimensions in the ITO environment was then introduced. The internal and external influences of risks were considered along with the behaviour of the risks over time.

It is therefore my hope that some of the concepts discussed in this book will be useful to the reader. Again, there is no substitute for experience, common sense and logical reasoning. The RDS, when employed in conjunction with all the concepts and ideas appearing in this book, should prove to be useful in understanding, measuring, illustrating and anticipating the risks that will ultimately become manifest in the ITO environment.

8

A case study – ITO risks

The case study presented here is about a multinational organization that has embarked on an ITO exercise, and which has been referred to already in several chapters of this book. It serves as a practical example that re-illustrates the concepts introduced earlier. Unlike the situation in other ITO exercises, the organization in this case study has an unusually high incidence of risk characteristics from environmental (political environment), business, and strategic risk dimensions. These dimensions are conspicuous set against the discussion on pure operational risks. This natural exaggeration is appropriate as it amplifies some of the concepts discussed in previous chapters and allows the details to be more clearly observed.

To protect the privacy of individuals and the organization, pseudonyms have been intentionally used for purposes of the case study. The data presented, however, are real. Actual data were collected by a team of individuals over a period of 5 months while working on the ITO exercise.

The team that worked on the project was one that would normally be found on an ITO exercise. It consisted mainly of personnel with a background in IT who had worked in the IT department prior to the exercise, and managers from every department in the organization. The Board and Senior Management team were the sponsors for the ITO programme. The project 'champion' was the Chief Information Officer (CIO) for the organization and she had the role of maintaining the focus of the team. She provided the 'energy' from the start of the ITO exercise to its completion. Although there are multiple facets of the ITO exercise that could be highlighted, only the risk capture and management activities are highlighted, as applicable to the subject matter in this book.

8.1 Case study background

The case study organization provides clinical investigative services for regional tertiary care centres (acute care hospitals). The services provided include the processing of samples, analysis and results reporting. To facilitate this, the organization has maintained an in-house IT function for over 10 years. In order to save costs and focus on its core competence the management team has recently decided to embark on an ambitious project to outsource all the major components of the IT function.

Clinical investigative services is a discipline within the healthcare industry that include both laboratory and radiology functions. Together, these functions require processes that are information intensive. Data are collated, stored and disseminated on every sample collected and results are reported and stored in the patients' medical records. Subsequently, the analysis and presentation of the outcomes of the tests also require significant use of the IT function. This forms one of the most important sources of current information for diagnosis by a clinician. The laboratory tests that are performed by the organization for its clients include those involving haematology, chemical pathology, cytology and microbiology. The various modalities covered in radiology include X-rays, CT scans, ultrasound and MRI. As such, the operations and reporting requirements are complex, and the accuracy and timeliness of the information provided are vital. Clients are predominantly healthcare centres including hospitals, clinics and centres for rehabilitative care and allied health, which are situated in geographically disparate locations spread over three time zones.

So, the organization itself is an outsourcing services supplier as it performs tests for outsourcing services buyers, the healthcare institutions. It is, however, also a buyer of outsourcing services. In this case, it is buying outsourcing services for its IT function. The risks in the IT function will be discussed here.

As a business entity, it needs to deliver value for its shareholders in the form of profitability and return on investment. Also, like any other business, it is not immune to pressures for cost reduction. As a professional services organization in the healthcare industry, the cost objective and expenditure priorities for patient safety and accuracy of information need to be balanced through a series of management activities that operate to maximize the efficiency of all the organization's resources.

In addition to industry pressures, the organization is subject to environmental influences – it has the added pressure from the Government to provide services at cost for many social projects including participation in operations relating to bio-terrorism; disease outbreaks; and more recently the avian flu epidemic that threatened the nation. To make matters worse, this organization was the only one in the country to have specialized facilities for selected medical tests. The need to collect, maintain and disseminate information through its IT function was distracting its people from the core business of providing medical testing services.

Finally, heightened competition in the industry had resulted in greater yield and price pressure on the organization's products and services. It had to re-engineer and urgently change (transform) current operations with attention to lowering operating costs and increasing margins through focus on customer care, improved services and increased reach. Competitive pressures provided the catalyst for change.

It had used contract workers to perform specific functions like the installation of the local area network (LAN) and short-term contractors to write small computer programs. The management team had devoted a significant amount of time to supervise and manage these contracts. The same team has now decided that its IT function is not a core competence function and that it wants only to benefit from the outcomes of this function[1]. It will outsource the IT operations along with the attendant operational risks. The IT operations, however, are strategically important to the organization because of the need for accurate and real-time information. This need to keep selected components (for example, the information on the Oracle™ database and electronic interfaces between some of the test machines and the computer system) of the IT function confidential and proprietary was recognized early. To satisfy both these requirements, the outsourcing supplier had to have a strategic relationship with this organization (see 'Outsourcing Partnerships/Contracts' in Chapter 1). Organizational boundaries between the ITO supplier and this organization would merge as the outsourcing and supplier organizations would share in the performance and outcomes of the very important IT function.

8.2 Risks identification

The organization was not immune to risks. In fact it would be subject to a very diverse and complex set of risks that would have to be managed and mitigated to allow the ITO project to proceed. The framework that was used to capture risks in the project was derived from work by Earl (1996), as described in Chapter 3, where the risk elements are mapped against the eight risk dimensions, as illustrated in Table 8.1 below. Each risk element is discovered through an interview process, which is described in

---

[1] See differences between contracting and outsourcing in Chapter 1

Table 8.1   Mapping common risk elements with risk dimensions

Risk elements (Source: Earl, 1996)

					Risk categories/Dimensions			
	Technical	Financial	Legal	Operational	Business	Environmental	Informational	Strategic
Possibility of weak management	✓	✓	✓	✓	✓	✓	✓	✓
Inexperienced staff				✓	✓	✓		✓
Business uncertainty		✓			✓		✓	✓
Outdated technology skills	✓			✓			✓	✓
Endemic uncertainty		✓	✓		✓	✓	✓	✓
Hidden costs		✓					✓	
Lack of organizational learning				✓				
Loss of innovative capacity	✓				✓	✓	✓	✓
Dangers of eternal triangle			✓	✓	✓			✓
Technological indivisibility	✓		✓	✓				✓
Fuzzy focus				✓		✓		✓

Table 8.2 Buyer risks in the ITO project (case study organization)

| | Major risk dimensions | | | | | | | |
| | Internal → | | | | | | → External | |
	Technical	Financial	Operational	Strategic	Legal	Informational	Business	Environmental
Environmental Influences								
Competitive pressure			✓	✓			✓	
Within the healthcare industry (clinical tests)								
Buyers				✓			✓	✓
Suppliers				✓				✓
Substitutes				✓	✓		✓	✓
New Entrants				✓		✓		✓
Nationalism, Politics, Structure						✓	✓	✓
Global Events						✓	✓	✓
Hedging against currency fluctuation			✓	✓				✓
Industry Practices								
Follow-the-leader phenomenon				✓			✓	
Using IT as a primary function (cf supporting role)		✓	✓	✓			✓	
Governance of IT within structure				✓	✓	✓		
Shorter planning cycles			✓	✓		✓		
Reasons for outsourcing IT								✓
Cost reduction		✓	✓	✓				
Improved customer service		✓	✓	✓				
Improved revenue generation		✓	✓	✓				
Speeding adoption of new technology	✓							

Matrix of assessment criteria (continued). Column headers appear on the facing page.

Criteria	C1	C2	C3	C4	C5	C6	C7
Improved integration with business partners		✓	✓	✓			
Improved security (regulatory requirements)		✓	✓	✓			
Sharing Information			✓	✓	✓		
Contract negotiation & ongoing governance		✓	✓	✓	✓		
Organization's operations (outsourced)							
Company's past 5 year track record	✓	✓	✓		✓		
Management team performance	✓	✓	✓		✓		
Company's strategic plans	✓	✓	✓				
Lack of information on risks	✓	✓	✓				
Budgeting and demand management	✓	✓	✓			✓	
Poor technical resources	✓	✓	✓		✓	✓	
Outsourcing all its IT operations	✓	✓	✓		✓	✓	✓
Working with a strategic IT outsourcing partner	✓	✓	✓		✓	✓	✓

the following section. The matrix also allows the risk elements to be verified against the risk categories and vice versa.

As elements are collected and each risk dimension is verified, the probability of occurrence and the magnitude of loss information are used to compute the risk exposure along each dimension. In addition, each risk dimension is related to a source of influence, whether internal or external to the organization. The source of the risk is identified early and documented for subsequent risk mitigation activity (see below).

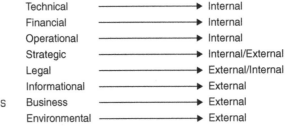

Figure 8.1
Sources of risks (risk dimension) mapping to sources of influence

Technical	Internal
Financial	Internal
Operational	Internal
Strategic	Internal/External
Legal	External/Internal
Informational	External
Business	External
Environmental	External

Once the risks elements can be confirmed, the probability of occurrence and severity levels can be determined to allow computation of the total risk exposure values.

The risk elements were grouped under three key headings: environmental influences, industry practices and the organization's operations (ITO exercise). Figure 8.2 shows the summary illustration of the matrix obtained from this case study. Some of the elements are further described here.

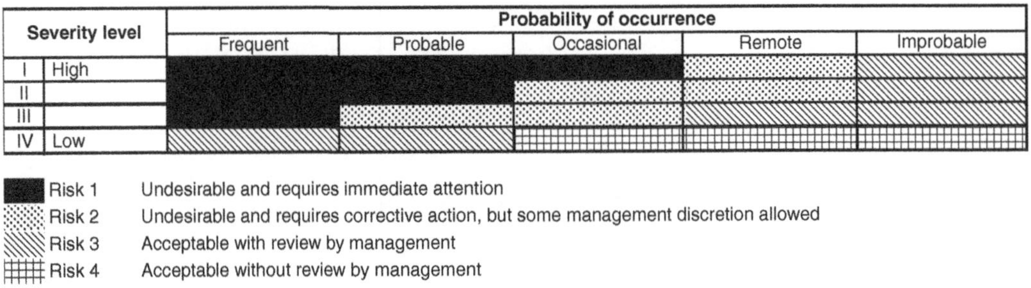

Severity level		Probability of occurrence				
		Frequent	Probable	Occasional	Remote	Improbable
I	High					
II						
III						
IV	Low					

Risk 1 Undesirable and requires immediate attention
Risk 2 Undesirable and requires corrective action, but some management discretion allowed
Risk 3 Acceptable with review by management
Risk 4 Acceptable without review by management

Source: US Government Accounting Office, 'Information Security Assessment – Practices of Leading Organizations', June 1999

Figure 8.2 Risk assessment matrix

8.3 Internal (endogenous[2]) risks

The organization in the case study, like others in the industry, carries high fixed costs, and experiences an unpredictable cash

---

[2] See also Figure 3.2 in Chapter 3

flow and low margins as a result of price competition and the inevitabilities of unforeseen regional and global events. The radical and strategic decision to outsource its IT function was based on three key factors: the need to focus on core competence, the need to reduce operational risks and the need to simultaneously derive optimal outcomes from the IT function at a lower cost.

Buyer risks

Operational risks were never really fully quantified, or were partially ignored as the management team never appeared to consider the effects of failure of the IT function. It had maintained a fully operational IT department with over 100 trained IT personnel. The first computerized application had been installed over 12 years ago. The management team wanted to reduce *technical risks* by working with an ITO partner who would guarantee the performance of the IT function and include updated technology.

The organization had incurred excessive expenditure on excess capacity that did not match up to returns. Burdened with a large operation and high capital costs in a plummeting global economy, the organization had huge cash outflows as a result of the purchase of new equipment for specialized testing. Obvious implications included difficulty in repaying its debts. There was poor evidence of increasing volumes of medical tests and management literally gambled on increasing demand and regional and global orders based on trends for long-term diseases such as hypertension, stress, and cancer. Despite this evidence, orders were confirmed for more new equipment (approximately 25% increase in testing capability) to be delivered over a 5-year period. Demand for medical tests from existing and new customer bases remained uncertain. The *financial risks* were mounting and the *strategic risks* were close to the organization's point of intolerance.

Supplier risks

Two prospective suppliers had been considered in the selection process. Subsequently, only one supplier[3] was selected to perform the ITO task for the complete IT function.

---

[3] There are models where multiple supplier organizations work together to provide ITO services (see Chapter 1)

Initially, during the selection and proposal consideration process, both suppliers were vying to win this potentially lucrative new business. The organization would outsource the major functional areas of IT including Cross-Platform Services, Help Desk Services, Mainframe Data Centre Computing, Midrange Data Centre Computing, Desktop Services, Network Services (voice and data), Application Development, Application Maintenance and Station Support (regional). The key strategic core activities to be retained by the management team would be the development, maintenance and control of IT strategy, IT policy and new solutions provision and systems integration. The Business Units would be accountable for business integration. Oddly also, given that mobile telephones, walkie-talkies and other equipment were under the control of the IT function, with the new structure, these were 'out of scope'.

The IT operation at the organization was logically separated into eight 'service towers'. These were functional areas that comprised multiple services: the Data Centre (mainframe, midrange and database) Processing Services, Network (server support) and Desktop Support Services, Help Desk Management Services, Application Management, Governance Services, Transition and Transformation Services, Business Continuity and Disaster Recovery Services, and Exit Management and Assistance Services. Each of these services towers had been derived from a previously created document from an exercise commissioned by the organization to identify key parts of the business.

The suppliers are familiar with the organization and its management. When bidding for the project, the immediate risk the suppliers accept includes a significant number of applications that have been unaccounted for or are unknown. This poses both a threat and a risk as the supplier would be bidding for an unknown quantity of work. This risk is classified as a *technical risk*. Also, there is a *financial risk* when there is competition for the work. The lowest bidder often wins the work but may be left to take on several unaccounted-for but contracted pieces of work that would quickly erode any profits (see Winner's Curse Phenomenon in Chapter 4). The load of *operational risks* would need to be covered when the transition from the buyer to the supplier takes place. The transition planning and governance of the project becomes a critical activity and is the responsibility of the supplier. The compensation for the supplier is the long-term, steady income stream that it begins to enjoy after the ITO project has commenced. Its *strategic risks* now need to be considered as other buyer organizations in the same industry area, for example, would be hesitant in allowing it to take over their IT function lest there be collusion or sharing of information (see also Agency Theory, Chapter 4 and Outsourcing Contracts, Chapter 1).

8.4 External (exogenous[4]) risks

The buyer and supplier organizations in the case study work in a similar environment and share some of the external risks and experience. The external risks typically derive from the legal framework, the environment, information availability and the business milieu.

Buyer risks

The *legal risks* to which the buyer is exposed stem directly from contract amendments that appear in almost all outsourcing contracts[5] as conditions change and the measurement criteria for outcomes of the IT function change (see Role of IT and the Productivity Paradox, Chapter 2). A governance process is implemented to ensure that flexibility in the contract takes the inevitable changes into account. This action mitigates the legal risks but does not cater for possible disputes and litigation, and possible service debasement.

As the buyer organization ventures into a new ITO exercise, it is exposed to regular *business risks*, which are much like the risks in any significant business venture. The ITO exercise is unique as it 'locks' the buyer and supplier into a long-term partnership and the business risks that are encountered will need to be managed even more meticulously. In addition, the risks from the *environment* change.

In this situation, the buyer organization also suspected that the suppliers had provided inaccurate information in an effort to win the bid. The exposure along the *information risk* dimension was not substantial but the risk of possible loss therefrom would lead to a threat of legal and financial risk.

Supplier risks

The suppliers on the other hand were facing a difficult time trying to differentiate their products and services offering. The IT function that was going to be outsourced was relatively generic

---

[4] See also Figure 3.2 in Chapter 3
[5] From the author's experience

and did not have many speciality services that would easily show that one supplier was better than the other.

Both organizations were large multinationals that had very significant technical expertise and capability, reputations for excellent service and solid track records to show that both were perfectly suited to manage the IT function for the buyer organization. Therefore only the price of the services to be contracted would tilt the decision in favour of one or the other.

The threat of *legal risks* was significant as the buyers would lock in to a long-term contract with the buyer and commit resources and time to deliver a set of very tangible outcomes that the buyer had already determined. In addition, the risk exposure along the *business risk* dimension was high given that the price of the services would be reduced significantly to beat the competition. The *environmental* and *informational risk* factors were very similar for both supplier organizations, which were operating under very similar sets of rules.

The risk dimension signature (RDS) would show the changes in risk profiles for the buyer as well as the two supplier organizations. This would also facilitate the negotiations process, which would be based on risks, resulting in a winning situation for all three parties. As risks are passed on from the buyer to the (winning) supplier, the buyer would need to adequately compensate the supplier as it would be interested in gaining the best outcomes. The supplier, on the other hand, would be forced to provide a reasonable price as it would need to clinch the deal. The criteria for the winning deal hence would be a relatively honest evaluation of the extent of risk that either supplier could tolerate for a reasonable outcomes set. In this situation, the larger of the two suppliers declined to bid citing unacceptable business and technical risks. It did not have a sufficient risk appetite to take on the work. The smaller, more nimble supplier organization had a higher risk appetite and was willing to take on more risks in the hope of gaining market share ahead of the competition.

The RDSs for both suppliers are constructed based on discussions and qualitative assessments made by representatives from the suppliers, together with input from the consulting team and buyer's project team. This formed the core business, or functional requirements, with the following core services:

- Cross-Platform Services
- Help Desk

- Mainframe Data Centre Computing
- Midrange Data Centre Computing
- Desktop Services
- Network Services (WAN and LAN)
- Application Maintenance and Development
- Disaster Recovery
- Organization Transformation Management
- Services to be retained by the buyer organization
- Facilities.

Arrangements by the buyer and supplier would also be carried out for the approach to the scope of services, definitive set of service levels, structure and management approach, roles and responsibilities, transition management, governance, long-term service approach and, finally, the value proposition as a target for the exercise. The human resources arrangements would include staffing plans and supplier personnel, who would be responsible for delivering the functionality required. The financial agreements would include an agreement on the term, pricing requirements and pricing structure, any retained expenses to be agreed and the transition services fees (which is often forgotten or omitted). The contractual considerations then also include all the items listed here but the details would carry the elements ranging from an agreement and description of the current environment, the buyer organization's requirements, a detailed description of the services to be provided, service level definitions and reporting requirements. Speciality requirements include software licensing agreements, voice and data network requirements (both domestic and international), the reporting and status requirements for activities that require development (i.e. work-in-progress requirements) and, finally, governance principles.

After all the components of the IT function have been outsourced, the remaining tasks that are 'left over' for the buyer organization include the critical components of the IT function, which are the IT policy and IT strategy, as well as the overview tasks for new systems selection, implementation and maintenance. This is illustrated in Figure 8.3 where the larger filled circles indicate greater responsibility. For example, the buyer organization's IT unit would still be responsible for the policy and strategy but not the systems implementation or maintenance.

The responsibilities of the buyer organization versus those of the supplier would need to be strategically delineated to deliver the maximum advantage to both parties. This, however,

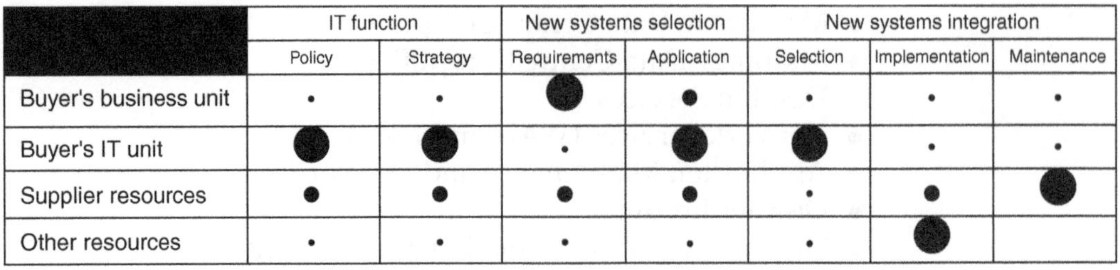

	IT function		New systems selection		New systems integration		
	Policy	Strategy	Requirements	Application	Selection	Implementation	Maintenance
Buyer's business unit	·	·	●	●	·	·	·
Buyer's IT unit	●	●	·	●	●	·	·
Supplier resources	●	●	●	●	·	●	●
Other resources	·	·	·	·	·	●	

Figure 8.3 Allocation of tasks between supplier and buyer (source: IT outsourcing project documentation)

exposes a number of key risk areas in the *strategic, business* and *informational* dimensions (referred to in the risks above).

The buyer organization would maintain primary accountability for its business units and the IT policies and overall IT strategy (see Figure 8.3). The IT requirements definition for the applications to be developed or purchased remains with the business unit and the buyer organization's core IT unit. After the outsourcing agreement has been agreed and is proceeding, the selection of the systems integrator also remains with the buyer organization. This is to ensure it retains the governance of the outsourced supplier. It still has control over, and overall responsibility for, the outcomes of all IT projects. The actual systems implementation and systems maintenance work is to be moved to the outsource supplier. In addition however, as illustrated in Figure 8.3, the supplier has a role of contributing to the decisions on IT policies and strategy and to other selection decisions.

8.5 Risk profiles from participants in individual and group sessions

The quantitative method was used in the previous section to derive one view of the risk profiles experienced by the buyer organization (buyer) as it engages with another organization (the supplier). A schematic of the methodology is also illustrated in Figure 8.4 initially proposed by Jones and Hunter (1995) for medical and health systems research. It has been adapted for use in the process discussed here. The method is straightforward where the 'Input' process will provide information for 'processing' and 'output' as an RDS profile.

The results of the analyses were subject to a lack of consensus by the participants and stakeholders primarily as a result of inconsistencies in perception, private agendas and hidden information.

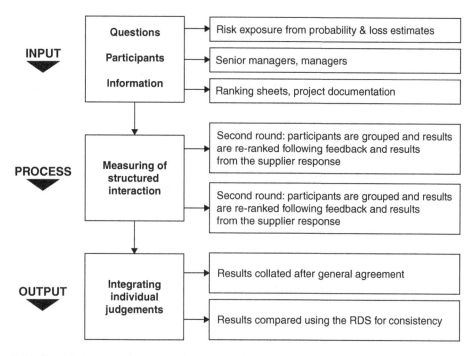

Figure 8.4 Qualitative survey methodology (adapted from Jones and Hunter, 1995)

This was expected. Selected individuals were given opportunities during individual and group sessions to allow the researcher to gain consensus on the risk 'readings'. The extent of agreement (consensus measurement) as well as resolution of disagreements (consensus development) were organized through a group facilitator. The discussions also provided a framework for qualitative assessment of evidence (though they are often concerned with deriving quantitative estimates from the evidence; for example, estimating probabilities for the risks experienced). The participants in the individual and group sessions comprised a selected group of individuals who represented the buyer organization's operations. The senior managers each represented a focus area in the buyer organization, and the senior manager from the IT department participated. The CIO, who was also an avid supporter of this exercise, selected each individual. The managers then also nominated participants. The exact numbers varied (and are identified prior to the results in the next section) but finally a pool of 38 participants was used.

The participants' main qualification was their knowledge of and involvement with the ITO decision and exercise. The initial meeting was called to explain what the research project consisted of and how it linked with the actual project activity to be conducted with the buyer organization. Each 'wave' of activity was also explained, as the RDS information would be collected at different points in time.

The main survey instrument was a questionnaire consisting of Likert scale ratings, asking the participants to rate the probability of occurrence and extent of loss that could be experienced by the buyer organization along the separate risk dimensions. Approximately half of the respondents were interviewed face-to-face, the other half via telephone or e-mail given the remoteness of the various sites. Minor editing was carried out for clarity and consistency. For the discussion questions, the responses were edited and discussed within the risk framework of the exercise since ideas, clarifications, and elaborations were required.

Various assumptions have been made and validated. A major assumption is that the exercises in this chapter adequately illustrate the use of a tool that enabled the collection of readily available information from both the supplier and buyer organizations to develop the risk profile at separate points in time: for example, the existence of direct internal and external influences on the pre-established risk dimensions for the ITO exercise at the buyer organization along the eight risk dimensions initially proposed. The relationship between the influences and risk dimensions is valid only if there are no other factors to be considered. This assumption is valid if the environment is controlled. In a dynamic business environment this may not hold true. The assumption nevertheless can be made based on the absence of any other input. The exercise hence can be said to provide some validity for the risk dimension and classification of risks.

Another major assumption is that the frameworks created by previous authors and researchers are adequate for the definition of risk exposure. It assumes that the work that has been done to date can be reused in this context and purpose. The risk exposure frameworks are extended and form the foundational elements of the RDS profile.

A further assumption is that the risk transfer mechanism is valid. When the operations are transferred from one organization to another, the nature of the risks is multidimensional. It is assumed that the risks do not actually physically move but are experienced by the party that takes over the activities that result in the risks.

Given the methods, processes and assumptions made in this chapter, the RDS profile was then used at several points in the activities timeline in the outsourcing of the IT function at the buyer organization. The various technical, financial, legal, operational, business, environmental, informational and strategic risk elements would be considered and changes observed.

8.6 Using the risk dimensions

The processes that were initiated to create an RDS profile have been carefully illustrated in this chapter. The 'subject', i.e. the buyer organization in the case study, for the creation of the risks profile, was selected to allow maximum opportunity to collate and process the risk information in an appropriate outsourcing environment. This allowed the researcher to be deeply involved with the daily activities that were linked directly to the decision to outsource the IT function, selection of the supplier organization, justification of the business case for the outsourcing exercise and engaging with the supplier in order to commence the outsourcing exercise.

The methods used allowed very detailed observations of the risks from perspectives intimate to the buyer organization and the specific ITO situation. The measurement scales were devised to allow the capture of risks from the eight selected, summary risk dimensions. All eight dimensions were verified against the causes and influences of risk both from within and external to the organization at the time of the readings. The processes involved required the gathering of data, and the processing of the information to provide meaningful risk exposure values, standardized with the use of a computer program written specifically to obtain the information sought. The program and the algorithms were subject to the regular software application tests.

In Chapter 2, some of the pertinent and existing concepts of risks inherent in an ITO project were illustrated. It was emphasized there that the IT environment was uniquely different given its rapid change and 'fluid' definition both as a supporting and a driving function within the organization in a competitive environment. Risks in this area included both operational and relationship risks. Further work by several researchers and practitioners suggested risk evaluation frameworks and others propounded a range of risk exposure measurement techniques for the ITO environment. The information at hand is therefore sufficiently substantiated to allow the risk profiles and the negotiations process to be addressed directly.

8.7 The buyer & supplier RDS profiles[6]

The results of the RDS tool comprised a risk profile for both the buyer and supplier organizations at predetermined points in time. Following this, the results of the RDS would be used to observe changes in the risk profile as the risk transfer phenomenon became manifest in the outsourcing exercise.

This evidence provides support for a comparison of the RDSs of two suppliers against what is perceived as an acceptable risk by both these organizations. It also provides confidence that the risk dimensioning is representative of the risks encountered. Movements and a presumed relationship between the risk dimensions provide early warning for both the supplier and buyer on possible outcomes and ways of mitigating risks.

At the start of the ITO exercise

The illustration in Figure 8.5 represents the RDS profiles for all the participants of the ITO exercise at two points in time. Point #1 was an RDS reading taken prior to the selection of the supplier. The risks elements were captured via the use of responses to a 'Request for Proposal' (RFP) document and material from the project. These were used in conjunction with the methods discussed earlier. At this juncture, the RDS profile for the buyer organization was also taken to assess the risk profile prior to the handover of the IT function to the suppliers, as well as to gauge the level of risks that were being experienced by all the participants of the ITO exercise. The difference in risk exposure between supplier S1 and supplier S2 is illustrated in Figure 8.6. The RDSs at point #1 were also used to form the basis of the negotiations between the parties.

After the conclusion of the selection process, that is at point #2, another RDS profile was taken only for the buyer organization. Point #2 was at a time when the ITO exercise was about to commence, after the selection of one successful supplier. The differences in the buyer organization's risk profile are shown in Figure 8.7.

When the risk profiles were being created and examined, an arbitrary 'acceptable' risk level of 3 was allocated to all the

---

[6] The supplier names have been withheld at the request of the buyer organization in the case study and arbitrarily named S1 and S2 for the purposes of this discussion

participating organizations. This would allow a benchmark to be established when the team members were interviewing the employees and stakeholders at both the buyer and supplier organizations for risk exposure values. For example, when level 3 was acceptable risk, then any number above this would indicate degrees of higher risk and any number below would indicate less risk or almost no risk to the organization. In Figure 8.5, for example, if the RDS profile for the suppliers were examined, then

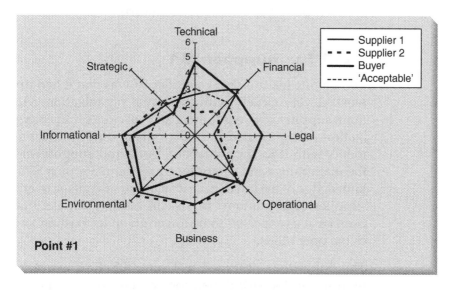

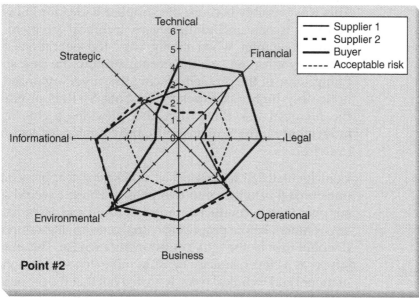

Figure 8.5 Buyer and suppliers' RDS data at point #1 (prior to the selection of the supplier) and at point #2 (after the supplier had been selected and the ITO exercise commenced)

the levels of legal risk exposure (along the legal risks dimension) for both suppliers S1 and S2 are very low and below the acceptable threshold for both organizations. The buyer organization, however, was experiencing unacceptable levels of legal risks as it was exposed to significantly more experience from the suppliers, who could potentially take advantage of the 'deal'.

For all three participants in the ITO exercise, the risk profiles at the time prior to the selection of the supplier organization, that is below point #1, are discussed in turn.

RDS for supplier S1

The unique feature about supplier S1 was that it had previously worked very closely with the buyer organization. S1 was the main supplier of IT equipment and services for the buyer organization and even had multiple outstanding contracting agreements with it to supply labour, parts and support services for the mainframes and computer equipment. Supplier S1's existing knowledge of the buyer gave it an unfair advantage over the other supplier organizations. Its risk in bidding for the outsourced exercise was expected to be lower given its existing knowledge of the operations.

The opposite is observed in Figure 8.5. Risk exposure scored high for all the risk dimensions except for strategic and legal. This was possibly because the supplier had prior knowledge of pending issues, including severe technical problem areas it would encounter when taking over the operations from the buyer organization (see the introduction to the case study outlining some of the problems facing the buyer organization). The noticeably high risk exposure (in both S1 RDS profiles) along the financial risk dimension also provides a clue as to S1's judgement on the propensity to make a financial loss from this exercise.

Coincidentally, S1 had proposed a preliminary approach to divide outsourcing activities into two phases. Phase 1 would allow the supplier time to conduct appropriate audit and assessment of the environment before proposing a final outsourcing solution. Phase II would then be the actual outsourcing exercise. This may be construed as a clever strategy by S1 to mitigate its operational, informational and technical risks. It turned out that the proposal would impose unacceptable business and operational risk on the buyer organization as the final supplier would have been selected and the bargaining power would have been diffused significantly.

To maintain a fair and unbiased process, the buyer organization had already carried an element of business and legal risk given its industry position nationally and degree of risk imposed by the Government. This also placed some stress on S1, which is conspicuous in the high risk exposure in the environmental risk dimension in Figure 8.5.

In addition, other environmental risks were very high. The reasons for this are not discernible from the RDS illustration in Figure 8.5, given the uncertainty in the domestic environment (as discussed earlier) as well as in the industrial sector with the onset of global terrorist activity (at the time of the case study in 2002), the regional SARS epidemic in 2003 and regional instability (in 2003/2004). This also affected business and operational risks. Some of the operational risks, however, were mitigated through the use of new equipment, better use of existing personnel and stringent checking procedures.

The relationship between S1 and existing local providers was also another risk factor. As S1 was an American organization, the risk was that it would have an insufficient track record with local vendors to attract local assistance should this be required[7]. For example, if the buyer organization had to work with a local transport organization that did not have a working relationship with S1, then this would place increased and undue pressure on the logistics of the buyer organization. This risk is environmental, and would have been unacceptable to the buyer organization and also to the supplier. Given the role of the buyer organization and its relationship with the Government, concerns over not being seen to be loyal to national interests by working with an organization located overseas also created risk in the environmental risks area, especially at a time when the threat of terrorist activity was high. The buyer organization had close links with the Government and it would have been politically incorrect to be seen as having little interest in the domestic scene. The risk exposure along the strategic risk dimensions was within acceptable limits. Again, this could be construed as a 'good account' for S1 as it would increase its market share in the outsourcing market in the country.

The supplier was to assume a position as a prime contractor and in this role it would be managing relationships with other

---

[7] Many IT components can be sourced locally, i.e. within the country; and local relationships would mean that the components could have been sourced at favourable rates and conditions

suppliers. S1 was a very large multinational IT organization. In this capacity, and in its ability to source for other suppliers, it was superior to many other organizations in the country. Noticeably, its technical risk exposure was within the bounds of what was considered acceptable.

S1 had a large legal team reviewing the contracts. Legal agreements and contracts bind the prime contractor with the buyer of outsourcing services. Other legal agreements and contracts bind the prime contractor with other contractors in back-to-back delivery promises. Penalty clauses would apply the appropriate pressure on the suppliers to comply. The RDS showed that risk exposure along the legal risks dimension was very low.

RDS for supplier S2

The RDS for supplier S2 was derived using a program similar to the one conducted for supplier S1, illustrated in Figure 8.5. In Figure 8.6, the RDSs for both S1 and S2 are illustrated simultaneously to allow a comparison between the two suppliers at the same point in time during the ITO exercise. Both the suppliers were competing for the same work.

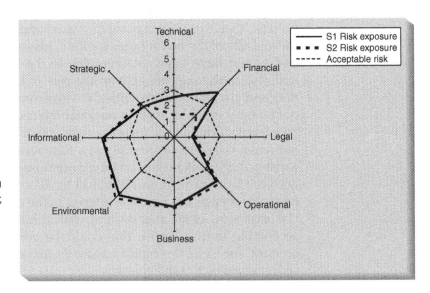

Figure 8.6
Suppliers' RDS data comparison at point #1 (similar to Figure 8.5 except that the buyer RDS has been removed for clarity)

The information from S2 is also unique. Although the RDS was constructed from interviews with six representatives from supplier S2 along with the supplier response to Request for Proposal (RFP) document, unlike S1, the people interviewed for S2 were not from the country (i.e. they flew into the country for this assignment only). This meant that their background knowledge of the buyer organization and working knowledge was obtained through literature and briefings from their local representatives. They would not have had the same working knowledge of the buyer environment and advantages as would the people from S1.

Like the RDS for S1, that for S2 indicated how the supplier would perceive the risk to the buyer organization. In this case, S2 had a fresh view of the buyer organization and did not have prior knowledge of the IT environment. It was not aware of the complexities or details of the troubles the buyer organization was experiencing. And it did not have the time or the resources to familiarize itself with the buyer organization's IT operations. (Over a 2-month period, the buyer organization had disseminated as much information as possible via briefing sessions and via multiple 'Question and Answer' sessions to provide information for both suppliers prior to the negotiations.)

Both the RDSs for S1 and S2 are compared on similar bases in Figure 8.6. On examination, the basic patterns for both signatures (RDSs) were seen to be fairly similar. This similarity in the signatures suggests that the perception of risk by both the suppliers was also fairly similar. This also implies that the information sessions that the buyer organization had conducted may have provided sufficient information to allow both the suppliers to have almost equal perception of the outsourcing exercise. In this case, a bias toward S1 by way of information and perception may have been minimized through extensive conversations with the supplier representatives during the exercise.

The risks in the operational, business, environmental, informational and strategic risk dimensions were almost the same for the two suppliers. Assuming that the suppliers S1 and S2 had no inherent advantage, this observation suggests validation of an earlier proposition wherein the relationship between the risk exposure and both internal and external influences on the two suppliers was consistent. The risks along the dimensions just mentioned were influenced by external factors.

Both S1 and S2 were placed in the same environment where the external influences, i.e. the buyer organization, environment and bidding structure (IT outsourcing project), were common for the two suppliers. If Figure 8.6 were reviewed again, the risk dimensions most affected by internal influences would be technical, financial and strategic. In Figure 8.6, the largest difference in risk exposure between S1 and S2 lies in the technical and financial risk dimensions.

The financial, technical and strategic risks are affected by supplier internal influences. The 'spike' in the financial dimension for both S1 and S2 could also point to an early warning for risks in the area of the budgeting and financial modelling that need to be done.

Equation (4.1) for total risk exposure derived in Chapter 4, the total Risk Exposure, $\rho\omega = \alpha$ [Σ(product of adjacent risk magnitudes)] is reused here. α is a constant with a value that is a function of the number of risk dimensions. The total risk exposure (rounded to the nearest decimal place for consistency with the data input) hence is computed for both S1 and S2 as Risk (S2) = 38.6, and Risk (S3) = 36.2.

The results also indicate that there is an almost equal risk exposure for the two suppliers that are working in the same environment with the same buyer organization. Despite the obvious differences in risk exposure along the technical and financial risk dimensions, the small differences in the other risk dimensions appear to compensate for these differences.

Acceptable risk exposure indicated by the fine dotted line in Figure 8.6, is computed as Risk (acceptable) = 25.4. Both suppliers appear to be 'over-exposed' by 52% and 42% respectively (see Table 8.3). This indicates a project that has 'high risk' and an inherent need to reduce risks in all the areas other than the legal, strategic and technical, wherein the suppliers appear to be most comfortable. The term high risk also presupposes the notion that the suppliers' appetites for risks are lower than the 42% over-exposure value computed.

Table 8.3 Risk exposure levels for S2, S3 against 'acceptable' risk

	Supplier S2	Supplier S3	Acceptable
Risk exposure	38.6	36.2	25.5
% Over-exposed	52	42	

Unacceptable risks occur in five of the eight dimensions identified in this exercise. From observation of the shapes of the RDSs, it appears that there is least exposure in the area of legal risks. If the theory that total risk exposure remains constant is true, the risk exposure along the legal risk dimensions can be used to compensate for over-exposure along the other risk dimensions;

i.e. this is a risk area where some trade-off can occur. Practically, this means that it is possible for legal instruments or agreements to be crafted and used to offset or reduce the informational, environmental and business risks. For example, the suppliers could arrange indemnity clauses, promising to deliver certain activities or deliver certain products in exchange for certain assurances in the business and environmental dimensions.

Qualitative assessment of the buyer RDS

The risk exposure (rounded to the nearest decimal place for consistency with the input data) for the buyer at point #1 is defined mathematically as $\rho\omega = 41.1$. This measurement derives from the risk exposure computation following the equation for total risk exposure derived in Chapter 4, where

$$\rho\omega \text{ (total risk exposure)} = \alpha \left[\Sigma \text{(product of adjacent risk magnitudes)} \right]$$

as also reused here. α, in this instance, is equal to 0.3536.

The acceptable risk exposure (marked by the dotted line in Figure 8.5), is Risk (acceptable) = 25.4. Through similar computation the Risk (maximum) = 101.8. A possible interpretation could be that the current risk profile is 15% over the acceptable risk tolerance level.

The least significant risks areas are business and strategic. All other areas appear to have risks that are unacceptably high. From the interactions with individuals at the buyer organization, the most prominent feature, which was repeatedly highlighted in the discussions, was concern that the buyer organization was in turmoil because of uncertainty in its industrial sector and in its current political setting. The environment was most significant to the outsourcing of the IT function as the suppliers were US companies and were subject to intense scrutiny from local government (being overseas companies). This was a unique risk situation, highlighted in this case with a very high reading for risk exposure along the environmental dimension.

Risk exposure along the informational risk dimension was a possibility because the IT infrastructure that supported the buyer organization's operations was almost non-functional. 'Systems are not integrated and other components practically not working' (CIO, personal communication, 5 November 2002). Operational risks were high generally as a result of poor information (i.e. late or incorrect information). This extended to high legal risks (from suits as a result of negligence). Technical risks were also high as a result of non-performance issues. Many of these issues, however, were interrelated. When the suppliers were invited to bid for the outsourcing exercise, each organization was assessed for its ability to deliver superior IT results for the buyer organization.

The buyer RDS profiles were measured at two points in time, point #1, i.e. when the suppliers were being selected, and point #2, i.e. when the ITO exercise had commenced using the supplier selected.

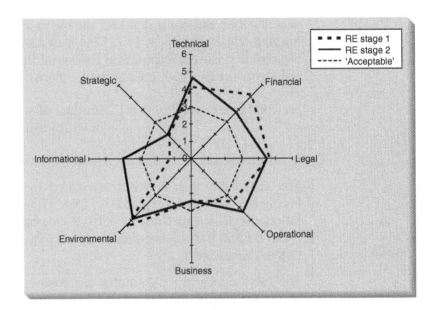

Figure 8.7
Buyer RDS data comparison at two points in the ITO exercise

Just after the commencement of the ITO exercise, the risk dimension signature for the buyer organization was tested again. This time around, the risks appeared to exist along similar dimensions but were manifest in different ways and in magnitude of exposure.

Many of the issues had already been addressed through joint working sessions where both the supplier and buyer teams had had thorough discussions and undergone exchange of documentation, and had completed due diligence with respect to each other's organization. Both parties were aware of the types of risk that were going to be 'passed-on' from the buyer to the supplier. Negotiations had already progressed to the stage when the supplier had also quoted its 'fee' for services to be rendered according to the agreed scope and scale of the exercise. The supplier's risks would have been taken into account already. This is referred to as point #2 for the purposes of measuring the RDS of the buyer.

There were sixteen selected participants from the buyer organization for this round of data collection. The CIO was in the group, together with eight senior general managers, and senior managers from the IT, audit and risk groups as well as from functional areas that utilize IT in routine operations.

The risk exposure computed at point #2 yields Risk (buyer @ pt 2) = 36.6 (see Figure 8.7) as compared to the previous risk exposure at point #1 (see previous section) of Risk (buyer @ pt 1) = 41.1. The risk exposure decreased along multiple risk dimensions. This confirms an earlier expectation that the total risk exposure would decrease as a result of selecting supplier S1. On examination, the topology of the RDS also illustrates a very dramatic reduction (from 4.1 to 1.3) in the informational risk dimension. With minimal contractual problems (see legal risk dimension), the buyer organization is expecting to reap the benefits through the supplier including economies of scale, scope or specialization in the form of improved quality, lower cost or faster time to market of all its operations, translating roughly into lower informational risks. This has also been observed in the literature (Quinn and Hilmer, 1994).

Some researchers observe lower informational risks where the supplier provides a multitude of easily measured activities that are specified in the service contract (Shachtman, 1998), allowing the buyer organization to generate greater outsourcing opportunities and stronger incentives for its partner (Holmstrom and Milgrom, 1991). The ability to monitor services from the IT function eases the monitoring exercise. This could explain the significant reduction in informational risk from the perspective of the monitoring dimension.

The buyer organization, unlike in a situation where there exists a large degree of uncertainty with respect to various factors of services provided and the external environment, faces a consistent environment wherein the IT components and functions have been long in use and are familiar to both supplier S1 and the buyer organization. Issues of poor monitoring raised by researchers such as Quinn and Hilmer (1994) are not as pronounced in this instance.

Uncertainty is a constant in IT-based processes, making outsourcing inherently difficult, owing to the expectation that current 'facts' will no longer be relevant soon after the commencement of a relationship. As the buyer organization is also trying to raise its IT capabilities, the uncertainty in the technical environment has also been de-emphasized. Indeed when the technical risk dimensions between point #1 and point #2 are compared, the technical risks have decreased as a result of uncertainty.

Supplier S1 had a high reputation for delivery and the perception was that it would deliver to the required standards. It was known that the losses from insufficient or inaccurate information as a result of poor performance from the IT function was high but the dramatic reduction in the probability and extent of loss as a result of the outsourcing of this function to supplier S1 was surprisingly high. The highest reduction in risk exposure among all the risk dimension changes was seen here.

The RDS topology at point #2 also looks rather dramatic, with an extremely acute angle for the environmental risk dimension (see Figure 8.7). This is probably misleading as the risks for those adjoining, informational and business, had decreased from unacceptable levels to within the acceptable risk limit of 3.0. Discussions at that time, however, revealed qualitative information that contributed to the significantly high environmental risks including information privy to the supplier only, i.e. asymmetries in intelligence information before contracting, imperfect monitoring of the supplier's actions, and external or exogenous changes that allow the supplier to behave opportunistically (see also Agency Theory in Chapter 4).

The levels of risk in the financial and legal risk dimensions appear to have increased as a result of the outsourcing activity. There are transactions costs associated with reliance on the market, including the explicit co-ordination costs and more complex contractual risks. This is evident in this exercise. Although the control over the outcomes has increased through contractual instruments, the mitigating factor was recourse through the legal system. This increased the anxiety levels of management and the perception of legal risks. Also, although the loss of control over the process itself was intentional, this was the point that was highlighted throughout the discussion and interview sessions; it had contributed to additional (or access) precautionary measures that raised the internal or endogenous influences that contribute to financial risks.

It is worthwhile noting that the outsourcing exercise had included a range of risk mitigating activity built into the governance contract as well as the service level agreements. A more meaningful observation would be if both the RDSs (points #1 and #2) were compared simultaneously.

Quantitative assessment of the buyer RDS

When both the RDSs are superimposed and compared, the differences as a result of the planning activity become more obvious. The illustrative comparison (Figure 8.7) clearly shows the changes in risk exposure between the measurement from point #1 to point #2. The percentage change in total risk exposure from 41.1 to 36.6 is measured against the maximum possible risk exposure, i.e. 101.8. By way of computation, this indicates a 4% reduction in total risk exposure.

Although this is a very rough measure of the total risk exposure, it also provides a perspective on the relative amount of change in the overall risk landscape that is being discussed. The buyer organization, it appears, is not expecting its risk profile to change significantly after the ITO exercise. In fact, if the topologies are compared, it is also obvious that some of the risks have increased along several critical dimensions, e.g. financial risks (see Figure 8.7).

The main difference is the change in risk exposure in the areas of financial and operational risk. The financial risks seemed to have escalated significantly (by 24%) through loss from unbudgeted events as a result of lack of experience and expertise on the part of the buyer organization's personnel in relation to the outsourcing activity. In addition, the general uncertainty in the budgeting process did not raise the confidence of the finance personnel or of the general managers in their various operational positions. The supplier was expected to take up the operational risks. This perception resulted in the lowering of operational risks (16% reduction). The biggest improvement noted from the RDS was the extreme improvement in informational risk (approximately 47%). This quantum leap corresponds to the buyer organization relinquishing operational control to the external party. This also implies that there was a significant lack of trust in the internal IT operations legacy in respect of delivering accurate and timely information.

In the previous section the total risk exposures between points #1 and #2 were compared instead of the risk profiles from the respective RDSs. If the difference between each individual risk dimension were compared to the 'acceptable' risk level of 3, the risk difference or risk variance between acceptable and actual risks would be obtained. The average difference between actual and acceptable risks in all the risk dimensions represents the level of risks above 'risk appetite' for the buyer organization. At the beginning of the exercise (point #1), the difference was quite significant (0.9 of 6.0), i.e. an average of about 15% over the tolerance limit. At the end of the negotiations and at the commencement of the contract with the supplier, the average risks dropped (0.6 of 6.0), i.e. an average of 10% over the tolerance limit. This 5% difference in average reduction in risk level, approaching 'acceptable' risk levels, was used to show that the decision of the buyer organization to outsource the IT function was indeed advantageous.

The industrial environment of the buyer organization is turbulent. Many buyer organizations install new systems in anticipation of external changes, with few data on the nature of change. Bounded rationality often impedes comprehensive contracting in these situations, resulting in contracts with misaligned incentives or significant changes in bargaining power, allowing the supplier to appropriate fees from the buyer. Contractual risks are greatest for those projects that are critical to the buyer organization's competitive advantage. These systems often provide the buyer with unique benefits that cannot be achieved without the contracted services. This trait increases the case study buyer organization reliance on supplier S1, increasing the possibility of supplier hold-up. The effects of these influences have been discussed extensively but appear, however, to cause minimal concern at the buyer organization, where an increase in legal risks is observed.

As mentioned before, supplier S1 has been working with the buyer organization in the capacity of hardware supplier. Concerns existed over the supplier's access to confidential data and processes that provided it with competitive advantage. A major objective of the outsourcing exercise, however, was to be able to leverage the supplier for its superior systems and processes. This element was de-emphasized as the concerns were borne by the supplier.

The financial risk dimension had increased. One observation relates to the interconnectedness of the exercise within the buyer organization. The exercise requires the supplier to be intimately familiar with procedures from various sources at the buyer organization that may be quite difficult to implement. The IT function affects multiple stakeholders within the buyer organization, making it difficult to specify desired requirements and functionality. A specific example is the standard operating PC environment (SOE-PC) where responsibility for the desktop is outsourced component-wise. Co-ordination difficulties and multiple standards in use throughout the buyer organization, plus peculiar levels of autonomy, increase the complexity. While internal IT providers may be generally familiar with the operations of an organization, data collection and the mastering of specific procedures throughout the organization by an outside vendor are costly and increase the overall levels of financial risks arising from uncertainty and scope creep.

8.8 Concluding remarks

The premise of the discussion on managing the risks of IT outsourcing began with a comment that this activity involved a combination of the art of management and the science of measuring an indefinite event, risk. The notion of capturing and illustrating risks with the RDS tool-set and interpreting the risk profiles was shown to provide the basis for measurement. Several theories were then used to assist in translating some of the characteristics of risk into predictable trends. With the rather lengthy discussion made in the past few pages, it is hoped that the reader gains an alternative view and a further appreciation of the use of the RDS and of the concepts where the risk dimensions share a relationship in any typical ITO project, and will see that the risks are indeed measurable and manageable.

The art of management of the risk events that occur then takes over as activities and programmes are put in to place to mitigate the effects of the risks, to manipulate the influences or origins of the risk events, and to control the internal and external factors that could result in events that in turn give rise to unwanted outcomes. There is no substitute for experience and the innate ability to manage an organization's resources, the environmental factors and the factors that influence other organizations in the same sector.

It is therefore my hope that the concepts introduced and tools that can be developed using the RDS will help in your current ITO exercise or the next time you are involved with an ITO exercise and activity.

References

Alexander, M. and Young, D. (1996) Strategic outsourcing. *Long Range Planning* **29** (1): 116–119.

Aubert, B.A., Patry, M. and Rivard, S. (1998) Assessing the Risk of IT Outsourcing, *Proceedings of the Thirty-First Hawaii International Conference on System Sciences (HICSS)*, IEEE, Hawaii.

Baker, G.L. and Gollub, J.P. (1990) *Chaotic Dynamics*. Cambridge University Press, London.

Bensaou, M. (1999) Portfolios of Buyer-Supplier Relationships. *Sloan Management Review* **40** (4): 35–44.

Blaxill, M.F. and Hout, T.M. (1991) The fallacy of the overhead quick fix. *Harvard Business Review* **69** (4): 93–101.

Boehm, B.W. (1991) Software Risk Management: Principles and Practices. *IEEE Software*, January 1991, pp. 32–42.

Brislin, R. (1999) Communicating Information about Culture and Personality in Formal Cross-Cultural Training Programs. *Personality and Person Perception Across Cultures*. Lawrence Erlbaum, Mahwah, New Jersey, pp. 255–277.

Caldwell, B. (1997) Why Outsource? – Some Organisations Find Switching Doesn't Lower Costs. *Information Week*, 659.

Carr, D.B. and Nicholson, W.L. (1988) A program for exploring four-dimensional data using stereo-ray glyphs, dimensional constraints, rotation, and masking. In W.S. Cleveland and M.E. McGill (eds), *Dynamic Graphics for Statistics*, Wassworth, Belmont, CA, pp. 309–329.

Clemons, E.K. (1995) Using scenario analysis to manage the strategic risks of reengineering. *Sloan Management Review* **36** (4): 61–71.

Clemons, E.K. (2000) The Build/Buy Battle – Balancing the risks and rewards of information serve outsourcing. *CIO Magazine* (1st December, 2000).

Currie, W.L. and Willcocks, L.P. (1997) *New Strategies in IT Outsourcing: Major Trends and Global Practice Report*. Business Intelligence Ltd, London (December, 1997).

DiRomualdo, A. and Gurbaxani, V. (1998) Strategic intent for IT outsourcing. *Sloan Management Review* **39** (4): 67–80.

Domberger, S. (1998) *The Contracting Organisation: A Strategic Guide to Outsourcing.* Oxford University Press, Oxford, UK.

Donner, S. (2001) KPMG's Risk Management Services. *KPMG LLP (June)*, New York, NY.

Drucker, P.F. (1995) *Managing in a Time of Great Change.* Butterworth–Heinemann.

Earl, M.J. (1996) The risks of outsourcing IT. *Sloan Management Review* **37** (3): 26–32.

Eisenhardt, K. (1989) Agency Theory: An Assessment and Review. *Academy of Management Review* **14** (1): 57–74.

Elfing, T. and Baven, G. (1994) Outsourcing technical services: stages of development. *Long Range Planning* **27** (5): 42–51.

Elitzur, R. and Wensley, A. (1997) Game theory as a tool for understanding information services outsourcing. *Journal of Information Technology* **12**: 45–60.

Evans, P. and Wurster, T.S. (2000) *Blown to Bits.* Harvard Business School Press, Boston, MA.

Fowler, A. (1997) How to outsource personnel. *People Management* (Feb 20, 1997): 40–42.

Goodridge, E. (2001) Outsourcing makes work for lawyers. *Information Week* [online] http://www.techweb.com/wire/story/TWB20010102S0004; accessed 15th April, 2003.

Hagedoorn, J. (1993) Understanding the rationale of strategic technology partnering: inter-organisational modes of cooperation and sectoral differences. *Strategic Management Journal* **14**: 371–385.

Hamel, G. and Prahalad, C.K. (1994) *Competing for the Future.* Harvard Business School Press, Boston, MA.

Hofstede, G. (1980) Motivation, leadership, and organizations: do American theories apply abroad? *Organizational Dynamics* (Summer, 1980).

Holmstrom, B. and Milgrom, P. (1991) Multitask principal-agent analysis: incentive contracts, asset ownership and job design. *Journal of Law, Economics and Organisations* **7** (2): 24–52.

Hoskisson, R., Johnson, R.A. and Moesel, D.D. (1994) Corporate divesture intensity in restructuring organisations: effects of governance, strategy, and performance. *Academy of Management Journal* **37**: 1207–1251.

Jones, J.M.G. and Hunter, D. (1995) Consensus methods for medical and health services research. *British Medical Journal* **311**: 376–380.

Kaplan, R.S. and Norton, D.P. (1996) *The Balanced Scorecard.* Harvard Business School Press, Boston, MA.

Keller, P.R. and Keller, M.M. (1993) *Visual Cues: Practical Data Visualization*. IEEE Press, New Jersey, p. 24.

Kern, T. and Willcocks, L. (2001) *The Relationship Advantage: Information Technologies, Sourcing and Management*. Oxford University Press, Oxford.

Kern, T., Willcocks, L.P. and van Heck, E. (2002) The winner's curse in IT outsourcing: strategies for avoiding relational trauma. *California Management Review* **44** (2): 6–24.

Lewis, T. and Sappington, D. (1991) Technological change and the boundaries of the organisation. *American Economic Review* (September): 887–900.

Lorenz, E.N. (1993) *The Essence of Chaos*, reprint edition (April 1996). University of Washington Press, USA.

Markides, C.C. and Williamson, P.J. (1994) Related diversification, core competences and corporate performance. *Strategic Management Journal* **15** (Special Issue, Summer): 149–165.

Markus, M.L. and Tanis, C. (2000) The organisation systems experience – from adoption to success. In R.W. Smud (ed.), *Framing the Domains of IT Research: Glimpsing the Future Through the Past*. Pinnaflex, Cincinnati, OH.

McMillan, J. (1992) *Games, Strategies and Managers*. Oxford University Press, New York, NY, p. 6.

Miller, G.A. (1994) Reprint of the magical number seven, plus or minus two: some limits on our capacity for processing information. *Psychological Review* **101**: 343–349.

Murphy, J. (2004) Management update: evaluating and mitigating Outsourcing risk. *Gartner Outsourcing Report* [online], http://www3.gartner.com/ps/asset_61461_1535.jsp; accessed 5th May, 2004.

Nash, J.F. (1951) Noncooperative Games. *Annals of Mathematics* **54**: 289–295.

Nash, J.F. (1953) Two-person cooperative games. *Econometrica* **21**: 128–140.

Nelson, P., Richmond, W. and Seidmann, A. (1996) Two dimensions of software acquisition. *Communications of the ACM* **39** (7): 29–35.

Porter, M.E. (1985) *The Competitive Advantage*. The Free Press, New York, NY.

Prahalad, C. and Hamel, G. (1990) The core competence of the corporation. *Harvard Business Review* **68** (3): 79–91.

Quinn, J.B. and Hilmer, F.G. (1994) Strategic outsourcing. *Sloan Management Review* **35** (4): 43–55.

Quinn, J.B. (1993) *The Intelligent Organisation*. The Free Press, New York, NY.

Roach, S.S. (1991) Services under siege – the restructuring imperative. *Harvard Business Review* **69** (5): 82–92.

Saunders, C., Gebelt, M. and Hu, Q. (1997) Achieving success in information systems outsourcing. *California Management Review* **39** (2): 63–79.

Schirripa, F. and Tecotsky, N. (2000) An optimal frontier. *The Journal of Portfolio Management* **26** (4): 29–40.

Shachtman, N. (1998) Measure success – careful metrics help businesses get what they need from their outsourcing deals. *Information Week* **706** (October 26, 1998).

Sherer, S. (1995) The Three Dimensions of Software Risk: Technical, Organisational, and Environmental. *HICSS Proceedings* (January 1995), IEEE Press, New Jersey, pp. 369–378.

Sobol, M. and Apte, U. (1998) Outsourcing practices and views of America's most effective IS users. In L.P. Willcocks and M.C. Lacity (eds), *Strategic Sourcing of Information Systems*, Wiley, Chichester.

Teng, J.T.C., Cheon, M.I. and Grover, V. (1995) Decisions to outsource information systems functions: testing a strategy-theoretic discrepancy model. *Decision Sciences* **26** (1): 75–103.

Tho, L.I. (2004) An investigation of the interaction between risk types in the outsourcing of the information technology function. Deakin University Thesis, Australia.

Venkatesan, R. (1992) Strategic sourcing: to make or not to make. *Harvard Business Review* **70** (6): p. 101.

Venkatraman, N. (1997) Beyond outsourcing: managing IT resources as a value centre. *Sloan Management Review* **38** (3): 51–64.

Index

Index

For Product Safety Concerns and Information please contact our EU
representative GPSR@taylorandfrancis.com Taylor & Francis Verlag GmbH,
Kaufingerstraße 24, 80331 München, Germany

Printed and bound by CPI Group (UK) Ltd, Croydon, CR0 4YY
08/05/2025
01864347-0007